THE

BOOK

OF

PATIENCE

A MORE PATIENT YOU

COURTNEY E. ACKERMAN

Adams Media
New York   London   Toronto   Sydney   New Delhi

Adams Media
An Imprint of Simon & Schuster, LLC
100 Technology Center Drive
Stoughton, Massachusetts 02072

First Adams Media trade paperback edition August 2021

ADAMS MEDIA and colophon are trademarks of Simon & Schuster, LLC.

For information about special discounts for bulk purchases, please contact Simon & Schuster Special Sales at 1-866-506-1949 or business@simonandschuster.com.

The Simon & Schuster Speakers Bureau can bring authors to your live event. For more information or to book an event contact the Simon & Schuster Speakers Bureau at 1-866-248-3049 or visit our website at www.simonspeakers.com.

Images © 123RF/Jozef Polc

Manufactured in the United States of America

3 2024

Library of Congress Cataloging-in-Publication Data has been applied for.

ISBN 978-1-5072-1659-0
ISBN 978-1-5072-1660-6 (ebook)

Introduction

Patience is more than just a virtue—it's the ability to stay mindful, calm, and collected through any circumstance. It's the intentional choice to stay in control of your mindset, and it's a well of strength that you can draw upon each day when you need it the most. Though it's not always easy to be patient when personal struggles and modern life's daily challenges leave you feeling frustrated and burnt out, *The Book of Patience* provides what you need to restore your sense of inner calm, whatever life throws your way.

Throughout the book, you'll find 250 unique ways to practice and build your peace, strength, and patience, including:

- Mindfulness exercises
- Daily habits
- Inspirational quotes
- Enlightening mantras
- Empowering affirmations
- Reflective questions
- And more...

No matter how you prefer to learn, build on, and practice skills, you'll find things that work for you in this book. From developing patience for yourself and your loved ones to truly cultivating a patient mind, body, and spirit, *The Book of Patience* teaches you what you need to know to overcome challenges—as well as spark inspiration, resilience, and joy in your life—anytime you need it.

✦

Nature does not hurry, yet everything is accomplished.

—LAO TZU
Chinese philosopher and founder of Taoism

Focus On the End Result

When working on your goals, whether it be for a short-term project or a long-term endeavor, it can be tough to make yourself be patient. This is because you're so focused on the next step that you lose sight of the big picture and instead feel drawn into the tension—or even anxiety—of waiting.

In this exercise, you will remind yourself of the end result or the state you will get to eventually.

1. Grab a pen and a piece of paper.
2. Write down what you're feeling impatient about now. For example, you might write, "I want to get my LSAT test results back right away. The waiting is killing me!"
3. Now, write down the end result of the situation; be as forward-thinking as you can. For example, you might write, "The end result of this situation is that I will become a successful lawyer. One day I will be happily practicing law, far away from this moment of impatience."
4. Take a minute or two to think about the end result. Visualize it in detail.
5. Now write a reminder to yourself to be patient. For the example here, you might write, "I'll get them when I get them. Worrying won't make my test results arrive any sooner."

You'll get to the end result either way, but you can make it a smoother and more positive experience by choosing to practice patience.

Delay Your Meal

This is a handy habit you can build into your daily life to enhance your patience. Practicing it regularly will help you become more patient with barely any effort!

Here's all you need to do:

Before each meal you eat, take a few seconds to look at and appreciate the food you have. Simply sit with your utensils on the plate or table in front of you, and look down at your food.

That's it! By simply taking a moment to see and appreciate your food, you are getting your brain used to waiting for something it wants. The more you do it, the less hasty your brain will be in all situations when it wants something *now*!

However, keep in mind:

- Taking pictures of your food doesn't count toward this time (sorry—you'll have to take a picture *then* wait a few seconds)!
- If you pray before a meal, add a few seconds of silence with your eyes open after you finish your prayer.

Basic Mantra for Patience

One of the best ways to create the traits you want in yourself is to use a mantra. Mantras are handy ways to insert the things you want into your everyday life, by keeping your goal or vision in sight through repetition and mindfulness. Mantras for patience are especially effective because they encourage waiting through the sheer practice of taking time to say them.

Here's a great mantra for becoming more patient:

Peace. Patience. Calm.

This mantra is short and sweet, but it can have a huge impact. Repeat this mantra while you meditate, when you practice yoga, when you engage in mindfulness, or just in quiet moments throughout your day. Over time, you'll find that you really feel more peace, more patience, and calmer in your day-to-day life.

✦

A man who is a master of patience is a master of everything else.

—GEORGE SAVILE
English writer and politician

What Would Happen
If You Chose to Be Patient?

This is a simple question, but it can have a powerful impact. When your mind starts overthinking at what feels like a million miles per minute, it's easy to forget that you have a choice in how you direct your thoughts.

If you're feeling anxious, tense, or rushed, ask yourself this question: "What would happen if I chose to be patient?"

Think about how the experience would change if you chose to be patient. What would your situation be like right now? What would your situation be like in the future? How would you feel looking back, when whatever you were feeling impatient about has come and gone?

You can't always choose what thoughts or feelings arise, but you can choose how to respond to them. Ask yourself this question and ponder your answer to work on building your sense of patience. If you have a journal, feel free to turn this question into a journal entry.

Say a Little Prayer for Patience

Regardless of how religious, spiritual, or skeptical you are, this exercise can work for everyone.

The next time you find yourself feeling impatient or in a hurry about something, pause and take a moment to say a prayer. If you've never prayed before, or you're not sure who or what to pray to, pick something that is interesting or meaningful to you—like a star, the universe, or a beloved pet that has passed on. What you're praying to doesn't matter—it's all about the act of praying and taking some time to welcome patience into your life.

Now, with a direction in mind, close your eyes and say a little prayer for patience. You might say, "Lord, please help me be more patient in this moment," "Universe, send me some patience," or "Fido, I'd really like to practice patience right now."

Say your prayer in earnest, no matter how silly you may feel, and send it out to its intended recipient.

Find Something Blue

Sometimes, all you need to be patient is a distraction or a direction for any wayward thoughts. Instead of focusing on negative feelings of impatience, give your brain a task to focus on.

If you're feeling impatient, hit the "pause button." Sit down or remain standing and be still for a moment. Send your gaze outward around you. Look from side to side, taking in the whole room or area that you are in. Your goal is simple: to find something blue.

If you quickly and easily find something blue, challenge yourself to find another thing in a different shade of blue. See how many you can find before you have to get up and move on with your day.

This exercise works because your mind likes being busy! You can use your brain's tendency toward being busy to your advantage, to spark patience whenever you need it.

✦

Learning patience can be a difficult experience, but once conquered you will find life is easier.

—CATHERINE PULSIFER
Canadian author of Wings of Wisdom

Write a Soothing Sentence

The act of writing has myriad positive outcomes—it's therapeutic, inspires self-improvement, sparks creativity, and much more. It's also a great tool to inspire patience because writing requires a certain degree of thoughtfulness, regardless of your writing mode.

If you'd like to shift your brain down into a lower gear, try writing a soothing sentence. Your sentence should use soothing words, bring up serene imagery, and make you feel calm and collected.

Try writing anything that comes to mind, whether it's describing a scene or just using calming words. You might write sentences like:

- "The moonlight reflected off the still surface of the pond."
- "The garden was quiet and peaceful."
- "The wind whispers softly through the gently swaying trees."

Even if you have no idea what pond, garden, or trees you are writing about, putting pen to paper (or fingers to keyboard) is an effective way to leave you feeling more patient and peaceful.

Count to Ten

This is a classic technique to feel more patient, calm, and collected when a strong emotion arises. It has typically been used to squash anger before it takes over, but it's also a great way to neutralize sudden feelings of frustration and impatience in the moment.

Use the following technique when you feel a sudden burst of impatience:

- Sit down or find something to lean against in order to feel supported.
- Close your eyes and take a deep breath.
- As you exhale, begin counting up from one. If you find yourself counting quickly, you can always use the "Mississippi" counting method (i.e., saying "Mississippi" between each number).
- When you get to ten, take another deep breath. As you exhale, open your eyes. Notice how you feel.

This simple method of counting to ten is a great way to ground yourself in the present moment and detach yourself from strong feelings of impatience. If you still feel impatient once you get to ten, try counting to twenty or even thirty.

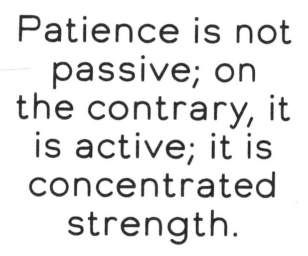

Patience is not passive; on the contrary, it is active; it is concentrated strength.

—EDWARD GEORGE BULWER-LYTTON
English writer and politician

Accept Feelings of Impatience

If you're feeling impatient and upset with yourself over it, try actively giving yourself a break. Instead of thinking something self-critical like, "I'm so bad at this, I can't even be patient for a moment!" try telling yourself, "It's perfectly normal to feel impatient sometimes, and this is one of those times."

You might find it difficult to go easy on yourself, especially if you're feeling swept up in negative feelings or challenging states of mind. However, you will likely find that acknowledging and accepting when you feel impatient can actually lead to greater patience.

Once you recognize that you are feeling impatient and accept impatience as an inevitable part of being human, you allow yourself to let go of the judgment. This takes away the extra burden you put on yourself, making space for self-compassion and peace.

Grin and Wear It

When you're feeling frustrated with your current circumstance, try smiling to naturally help yourself find some peace and patience. Smiling is a universal sign of positive feelings in virtually every culture. It also sends signals to your own brain that you are content and at peace. Use this biological fact to your advantage the next time you feel impatient.

Here's how to do it:

- Find a mirror if there is one nearby. If there isn't a mirror handy, you can still do the exercise; you'll just need to use some imagination!
- Standing in front of the mirror, take a moment to study your reflection. Move your attention to your mouth and notice how it looks with a neutral expression.
- Now, begin to smile. Move slowly, watching as your mouth curves upward. Try to make the smile look as natural as possible.
- Once you have a natural smile that feels good on your face, hold it for at least thirty seconds.

As you hold the smile, you might notice that you start to feel calmer, more collected, and more at ease, which naturally helps you be more patient.

Lie on the Floor

Sometimes, all you need for more patience in your life is a new perspective—literally! Try lying on the floor to take yourself out of your comfort zone, engage your creativity, and force a new perspective. You'll be able to get out of your head and any impatient thoughts you were having, and back into the present moment.

Don't be shy—give it a shot! Here's how:

1. Find some space on a clean floor, enough for you to stretch out on.
2. Lie down on your back. Stretch your arms and legs out, taking up some space.
3. Look up at the ceiling. Are there cracks you hadn't noticed before? Maybe spots with some extra paint? Spiderwebs?
4. Look around you. What else do you see that you normally don't? Dust under the couch or the bed? Socks lost behind some furniture?
5. Stay here for a minute or two, just enjoying the break and looking around you.

When you get up, remind yourself that your normal, everyday perspective is narrow. Taking time to patiently lie on the floor helps you see things you normally don't, and taking a step back and out of your own head can also help you gain a new perspective.

✦

Patience is the ornament of the brave. Patience is the real badge of courage; it is equally the mark of love.

—EKNATH EASWARAN
*Indian spiritual teacher, author, and translator
and interpreter of religious texts*

Show Yourself Some Gratitude

Showing gratitude to others is a social courtesy that's often impressed upon you in childhood. It's great to show your gratitude to others, but sometimes you may forget a vital component of gratitude: giving *yourself* gratitude. While self-gratitude inspires a greater capacity for love and generosity, it also sparks self-patience. When you thank yourself for the good and kind things you've done, you give yourself more space to wait, to be centered, and to be patient.

To try giving yourself some gratitude, list the good things you have done for yourself today. This can include things like cleaning yourself (e.g., taking a shower), nourishing your body (e.g., eating a good meal), and taking time to relax (e.g., reading a book). Thank yourself for each act of self-gratitude today and accept the renewed feelings of patience for yourself.

Look at Your Hands

When you're feeling stressed, it's easy to hyper focus on negative aspects of your current circumstance. When you need to get your impatient thoughts under control, put your sight to good use by focusing in on something that is easy to see: your hands.

Your hands are truly amazing things. You use them constantly to get through your day. Sometimes, you use them for big things, like lifting, carrying, and driving. Sometimes, you use them for the finer motions, like writing, typing, or giving a loving and gentle touch. It's really quite astonishing how much people do with their hands, yet how little time they spend acknowledging them.

To calm your mind and bring patience, take a minute to study them. Look at your palms and your fingertips. Notice all the delicate lines tracing your skin. Follow the lines up your palm, across your hand, and around your fingers.

Look at the backs of your hands. See the crisscrossing veins and notice the tendons that travel up to your knuckles. See the little wrinkles at each finger joint.

Think about how amazingly perfect each of your hands is, and how they allow you to live your daily life. Welcome any feelings of patience that come during and after this exercise.

◆

Patience is not the ability to wait but the ability to keep a good attitude while waiting.

—JOYCE MEYER
American author and president of Joyce Meyer Ministries

Compare to the Past

In today's modern world, it can be both a blessing and a curse to live in a world of instant gratification. It's great to get what you want, when you want it, with the right app. But current technology has made it more difficult to be patient when you can't get what you want on demand. To remind yourself of your ability to wait, try comparing your present to the past.

Imagine a moment in time, one that is at least twenty years in the past, but the further back, the better. Think about how long you would have had to wait for whatever it is you're waiting for now. For instance, if you're feeling impatient about receiving a reply to an email, imagine having to wait for a fax, a telegram, or even a handwritten and horse-delivered letter.

Think about how much more patient humans needed to be before the current days of quick satisfaction. Remind yourself that humans survived far more frequent and far longer waiting periods in the past, and that you can survive your current feelings of impatience too.

Squeeze a Stress Ball

Stress balls are an excellent tool for a variety of purposes, including bringing more patience to your current mindset. Whenever you turn your attention toward something *other* than the big, difficult thing you are struggling with, you create room for yourself. This room allows you to distract yourself from, and ultimately reduce, any impatience you are feeling.

So grab your stress ball and get to squeezing! You might find that a steady grip with continuous pressure is most helpful, or you might find that pulsing your grip helps you feel calmer and more collected. Don't forget that you have other options too: You can toss the ball back and forth, throw it into the air and catch it, or even roll it up and down the desk or your legs. Any of these movements will help you get your mind off the unpleasant experience of impatience and onto the tactile experience you are creating for yourself.

The two most powerful warriors are patience and time.

—LEO TOLSTOY
Russian author

Blow a Big, Round Bubble

Chewing bubble gum can be a helpful distraction from whatever is bothering you in the moment, including the frustrating feeling of impatience. It can also be a way to inject a little fun into the moment, and feel less stressed and more carefree. Make sure you pick up some gum you like so you have it on hand when you find you want to distract from impatience.

Pop a piece of the gum when you want to work on being more patient. As you chew, savor the flavor. Notice how it feels as you process the gum from a stiff, dry little stick into a moist, chewy, and somehow delightful mass.

As you prepare to blow a bubble, think about the feelings that come with it. Remember how it felt to blow bubbles as a kid. Remember the odd sort of competitiveness you had with yourself as you attempted to blow an even bigger bubble each time. Capture that sense of carefree fun as you blow a bubble now.

Best of all, savor the feeling of your impatience dissipating with every pop of your bubble!

Count Your Blessings

A surefire way to conjure up more patience in your life is to count your blessings. When you take time to acknowledge the good things in your life, it makes it difficult to focus on the bad things. Counting the good aspects in your life takes up mental energy, leaving little room for dwelling on negative aspects. Instead of thinking "I can't wait for [thing I'm impatient about] a single second longer!" you can take up space in your mind with "I'm so fortunate to have X, Y, and Z things in my life!"

Here's how to be more patient by counting your blessings:

1. Challenge yourself to come up with at least five blessings or good things in your life right now. You might count things like having a job that allows you to support yourself, a new TV series that you started watching, or the beautiful summer sun overhead.
2. Say them out loud, write them down, or just note them in your head. Spend at least a moment on each one, cultivating a sense of gratitude for it.
3. If you can easily come up with five, keep going as long as it comes naturally to you. Remember to keep count.

Revisit your mental list of blessings frequently for more gratitude, happiness, and patience in your daily life.

Brush Your Teeth at Quarter Speed

To get better at something, you have to practice. This is true of pretty much all skills, and cultivating patience is no exception. To become more patient, try actively choosing patience in more situations, especially ones where you don't necessarily *need* to be more patient.

One great practice is to slow it down when you brush your teeth. If you're like most people, you speed through brushing your teeth and your mind is far away, thinking about other things. Instead of your usual routine, try brushing your teeth at quarter speed; in other words, take four times longer to brush your teeth than you do normally.

While you slowly brush your teeth, making sure to reach every corner and crevice, focus your attention on the task at hand. Commit to doing an excellent job at brushing your teeth. Tell yourself it's worth taking the time to do something well.

This will only take a few minutes a day, but it will help you build up your patience over time so that you can apply that patience to all aspects of your life.

◆

One moment of patience may ward off great disaster. One moment of impatience may ruin a whole life.

—CHINESE PROVERB

Look in the Mirror with Love

It's not always easy to be kind to yourself, especially when you're feeling impatient with yourself. If you're too self-critical about your personal journey, it can be tough to let go of the judgment, and even harder to work on fixing the initial impatience.

If you notice that you have little patience for your own perceived flaws, focus on letting go of the judgment and accepting yourself first, then you can go back to working on increasing your patience.

Here's one way to do that:

- Find a mirror and stand in front of it. Put on soft lighting if you can.
- Look at your face, and really see it. Note the curve of your cheek, the way your lips naturally sit, and the brightness of your eyes.
- Remind yourself that this person you're looking at is worthy of love and acceptance. Cultivate feelings of love and acceptance, and offer them to the person in the mirror.

When you approach problems from a place of self-doubt or even self-dislike, it's really tough to make a positive change. Decide to approach from a place of self-love, and you'll find it far easier to improve yourself and welcome patience for yourself into your life.

Send a Friend a Text

A great way to work on becoming more patient is through your personal relationships.

Talk to a friend about your goal and set up a system: If you're struggling in the moment to stay patient, you will send a text to your friend reminding yourself to be patient and holding yourself accountable for being patient.

Here's a sample text you might plan on sending when you want to practice being more patient: "[Friend's name], I'm texting you because I'm feeling impatient and I want to work on it. As we discussed, I'm reaching out to say that I'm choosing to be more patient in this moment, even if it's difficult. Thanks for helping me stay accountable."

It's not your friend's job to reassure you or encourage you to be more patient, although of course they can if they'd like to. The text is all about your commitment to your goal. This method is a great way to keep you accountable for any change in behavior, including being less impatient.

◆

Rivers know this: There is no hurry. We shall get there some day.

—A.A. MILNE
English author of the Winnie-the-Pooh books

Do Some Tree Watching

The next time you are struggling with staying patient, look around you and find a tree. Trees are ubiquitous. Just about everywhere that people live, there are trees growing. Of course, they can look very different depending on location, but whether you look out your window and see palm trees or evergreen trees, you can use trees to be more mindful and more patient.

Once you find one, focus all of your attention on it. Ask yourself questions like the following to keep your mind on it:

1. What kind of tree do I think it is?
2. Does it have leaves or needles?
3. Does it lose its leaves or needles seasonally or is it always green?
4. What does that tree probably smell like?
5. Are the branches moving? Is it windy?
6. I wonder what creatures might live in that tree?

Basically, adopt an avid interest in the tree you see, even if it's just for a minute or two. Taking all of your attention and focusing it on this calming and relaxing task will help you stay more patient in the moment, take your mind off of whatever was making you feel impatient, and you might even get the added bonus of learning something new about your tree of choice!

Take a Few Deep Breaths

One of the most basic, tried-and-true methods of gaining patience is through breathing. Breathing is a fundamental component of being human. It's like your heart beating in that it's a mostly unconscious thing that keeps you alive, but it does differ from involuntary functions like heartbeats and blood flow—you can choose to consciously control it.

According to practitioners of meditation, yoga, and other breath-focused practices and lifestyles, the breath is your foundation. It is ever present, something you can always turn to when you need to ground yourself.

When you're having trouble waiting for something, try anchoring yourself in the present moment with the breath. Here's how:

- Close your eyes if you can safely do so.
- Take a deep breath, the biggest one you've taken all day. Fill your lungs completely.
- Exhale completely, allowing all the air to leave your lungs.
- Take just a moment to pause at the end, with your lungs empty. Rest in stillness. Repeat the deep breath in and out three more times.

Welcome the calmer, refreshed, and more patient state of mind, and remain still for a few more moments before getting back to what you were doing before.

Give Your Hands a Squeeze

You can put your hands to good use when you are feeling stressed, anxious, or impatient. You might read about or see people "wringing their hands" when they're troubled; this is because it's a surprisingly good way to manage feelings of tension. When you stay present and choose to do it mindfully, you can use your hands to lower stress, but also spark patience whenever you need it.

If you're feeling stressed and impatient, try giving your hands a squeeze. Follow these instructions:

1. First, use your dominant hand to grasp your non-dominant hand, your thumb reaching under the palm and your fingers wrapping around the back of your non-dominant hand, and give it a squeeze. Use firm pressure, but not so much that it feels uncomfortable.
2. Switch your hands and squeeze your dominant hand with your non-dominant hand.
3. Now bring your palms together, hands perpendicular to one another. Your fingers on one hand should be gripping the area between your thumb and pointer finger, and that thumb should be curling over the other. Squeeze gently.
4. Switch your grip so the other hand and thumb are on top, and give your hands another squeeze.

Use this method of squeezing your hands whenever you feel any tension or impatience for a convenient way to calm your body and your mind.

Close Your Eyes and Open Your Ears

Another great trick for bringing more patience into your life during difficult moments is to put all of your awareness into one of your senses. In this case, you'll put all of your awareness into your sense of hearing.

Follow these instructions to give it a try:

1. Find somewhere to sit down first. You don't want to get hurt trying this technique!
2. Get comfortable and close your eyes. Imagine "opening your ears," allowing all the sounds around you to enter your consciousness.
3. Now, focus all of your awareness and attention on what you hear. Notice each of the sounds you can hear.
4. Separate out the sounds and note each one individually. Label each one. For example, you might think, "That's a bird chirping. That's the wind rustling leaves in a tree. That's a person laughing."
5. Allow yourself to get lost in the sounds you are hearing. Experience them fully.

The longer you spend focusing on each individual and separate sound, the more in tune you'll feel with the present moment. Carve out time in your schedule to regularly listen to your surroundings to build up both your patience and your general awareness.

Take a Long, Hot Shower

To help you pass some time and find more patience, treat yourself to a nice long, hot shower. Don't worry about how long you spend in there or how much hot water you use (this time, at least!). Just give yourself permission to relax and enjoy it.

Showers are versatile. They're of course an effective method of getting clean, but they're also a great pastime if you feel stuck waiting awhile for something, and they're a great way to help you feel calmer and more relaxed.

Here are some ways to kick your relaxing shower up a notch:

- Use a fancy face or body scrub.
- Use a new shower gel or bar of soap.
- Try leaving your conditioner in for an extra minute or two to get silky smooth hair.
- Pause for a moment, close your eyes, and take several big, deep breaths, letting the steam soothe your lungs.
- Tilt your face up to the showerhead and let the water give you a face massage.

When you're ready, exit the shower feeling more refreshed, both physically and mentally, and try to apply your calmer state of mind to any feelings of impatience you had before your shower.

◆

Have patience with all things, but chiefly have patience with yourself. Do not lose courage in considering your own imperfections, but instantly set about remedying them—every day begin the task anew.

—SAINT FRANCIS DE SALES
Catholic bishop of Geneva

Play with Dragon's Breath

This exercise can be used whenever you need a boost of energy to distract you from impatience, or conversely, when you need to focus in on a task that you're impatient to wrap up. Dragon's breath is a fun breathing technique that wakes you up, shakes you up, and brings you powerfully into the present moment.

Here's how it works:

1. Find a comfortable seat and settle in. Sit with your feet on the floor or cross-legged. Rest your hands on your belly.
2. Start by breathing in normally through your nose.
3. Exhale forcefully through your nose. As you exhale, suck your stomach in toward your spine, using your hands to provide a gentle push.
4. Continue for at least one or two minutes, breathing in normally and focusing on your forceful exhale. If you get off track or tired, go ahead and take a quick break, then return to it.

At the end of this exercise, you should feel energetic and focused at the same time. It helps you feel engaged, eliminating any uncomfortable jittery feelings caused by impatience, and also centering and grounding you in the present moment.

Pet a Puppy

A wonderful and fun method of feeling more patient is to pet a puppy! Who doesn't like puppies? They're cute, cuddly, and they can literally give you a rush of feel-good chemicals when you interact with them.

Playing with a dog can boost your dopamine, serotonin, and/or oxytocin—chemicals that make you feel happier and more connected. Use this fact to your advantage when you're struggling for any reason. Plus, playing with a puppy requires patience if the puppy tends to get into mischief (as most puppies do!). Carefully watch the puppy and make sure it's playing safely with its toys and any other people, letting go of all other worries and impatience.

Of course, it doesn't have to be a puppy. A kitten works just as well, as do fully grown dogs, cats, or any other cuddly creatures you might have around the house. If you don't have a furry pet to love on, you can even use a stuffed animal or a soft blanket to get a similar cozy feeling—although it's certainly not as fun!

Whether you want to feel more relaxed, happier, or more patient, give petting something soft and fuzzy a try.

Press on Your Third Eye

If you're feeling tense and struggling to be patient, try pressing on your third eye. The third eye is an important pressure point in your forehead. You can think of it as a "button" of sorts, one that can be pressed to help you more effectively deal with difficult situations or negative emotions. It can also help you focus, keep you centered, and bring you into the present moment—all things that contribute to greater patience.

Try this method:

1. Find a comfortable seat and take a deep breath in to begin.
2. Put your palms together in front of your heart. Press in on your palms, putting gentle pressure against each hand. Now, raise your right hand slowly up to your face.
3. Take your pointer finger and place it on your third eye. This is a spot in the center of your forehead, about an inch above your eyebrows.
4. Keep your eyes open and press gently into your third eye with your finger. Feel your third eye opening under your finger.

With your third eye opening, you may feel a surge of calm and contentment. Open yourself up to it, allowing your third eye to help you be more patient in the moment.

Write Yourself a Note

If you're feeling overwhelmed by your current tasks and impatient to get them all done, you may accidentally miss a step. When you carry around all of your thoughts and feelings, you put pressure on yourself to remember them, which can make your mind feel cluttered and overly hasty to get everything out of the way.

Writing things down is a sure way to organize your mind. Also, the act of writing them down gives you some time to make space for yourself to breathe. Instead of letting your mind get (or stay) cluttered, try writing yourself a note.

Here's what to do:

1. Grab a piece of paper or a notebook and something to write with. Typing things out can be helpful, but nothing works as well as physically writing it down.
2. Write yourself a note about whatever your mind is stuck on right now. Write about the thing (or things) you're worried about, the things you need to remember for later, or the list of things you need to get done.
3. As an example, you might write something like, "I'm feeling overwhelmed by my responsibilities and I feel like I have a million things to do. I have to do X, Y, and Z today."
4. Simply writing down how you're feeling allows you to pause, to take a breath, and to let things go.

You'll find that the quick act of writing yourself a note about what you're dealing with right now will ease the pressure and make you feel calmer, which makes it easier to practice patience.

Tap In to Your Heart Center

Tapping in to your heart center is a helpful trick to bring peace and contentment, making it much easier to be patient without negative emotions getting in the way. While this move will feel familiar to a practitioner of yoga or meditation, it's a helpful trick for everyone, no matter how many times they've done it.

Here's how to tap in to your heart center:

1. Find a comfortable seated position and settle in.
2. Close your eyes and bring your hands together in front of your chest. Face your palms toward each other and press gently, putting even pressure on each hand.
3. Keep your back straight and upright, and bring your thumbs to rest gently on your sternum. Think about bringing your heart center up to meet your thumbs.
4. Take a moment to connect with your heart. Think about how you're feeling right now, what you want, and what you need. Give your heart some gratitude for continuing to beat, keeping your body alive and moving.
5. Tap in to the contentment you find there, and apply it to your current situation.
6. Open your eyes and feel that contentment slip into place, allowing you to feel more patient—both with yourself and with any situations that were stressing you out.

◆

Praise and blame, gain and loss, pleasure and sorrow come and go like the wind. To be happy, rest like a great tree in the midst of them all.

—GAUTAMA BUDDHA
Indian philosopher and founder of Buddhism

Give Yourself a Hug

If you're feeling impatient and insecure about anything at all, try giving yourself a hug! Hugs are a fantastic source of pleasure, warmth, and connection. Humans use hugs to show love and care for one another, to form and maintain social bonds, and to give and receive support. Hugs can do it all—they're kind of magical that way.

You might think that hugs are pretty great, but that doesn't help you when there's no one around to hug. But think again! Hugs are so magical that even hugs with only one participant can be effective in boosting your spirits and soothing your troubled mind.

Here's how to give yourself a hug and find some peace and patience along the way:

1. Make sure you have some space around you. Open your arms out wide. Imagine how you might open your arms to hug a loved one you haven't seen in a long time.
2. Now wrap your arms around yourself, placing your hands either on opposite sides of your back or gently gripping your opposite arm.
3. Lean into the hug, allowing yourself to feel the warmth of your own embrace. Give yourself a squeeze. Rock side to side a bit if that feels right.
4. Rest here for a moment, enjoying the hug. Tell yourself that you're doing the best you can, and that this is enough.

Stay in the hugging position for as long as you need, engaging in positive self-talk until you are able to feel patience and compassion for yourself, your growth, and your journey.

Find Three Good Things Around You

This is a classic exercise used by self-help professionals for years to help you feel more positive, collected, and patient when you're stressed or anxious. By choosing to look for the positive, you're telling your brain that it's safe and secure, and that there's no need to rush.

Follow these instructions to try this technique:

1. Find stillness wherever you currently are. Stop and look around you.
2. Challenge yourself to find three "good things." The definition of "good things" is open to your interpretation, but think of things that make you feel happy, inspired, or encouraged.
3. Note each thing you see and dwell on it for a moment. For example, you might see a picture of you and a loved one in your immediate vicinity. Take a moment to simply sit and look at the picture, and think about how much this person means to you and how glad you are to have them in your life.

If you found three things easily, keep going as long as you'd like! There's no limit to how many good things you can find if you look for them. Spend time focusing on everything good surrounding you, and let go of the entire thought process that was making you feel impatient, so that when you return to what you were doing, you'll bring your new positive and patient energy to your task.

Listen to Your Favorite Song

Music is a powerful tool that you can use for a wide variety of purposes, including enhancing your ability to focus and be patient. No matter what your favorite genre is—gentle classical or fast-paced hard rock—your brain finds it comforting to hear a favorite tune, and a comforted brain is much better at producing feelings of peace and practicing patience!

If you're feeling impatient, try finding your favorite song on your phone or laptop and turning up the volume. As you listen to it, focus all of your attention on it. Challenge yourself to being aware and present for every second of the experience. You can even put it on repeat a few times for maximum enjoyment.

If you find your mind starts to wander, focus in on one aspect of the song, like the sound of a particular instrument or the familiar lyrics. Sing it out loud or in your head to really tap in to the moment. When the song is over, savor the feelings the song inspired in you. Feel free to return to your tasks while listening to music, and if you're feeling impatient at all again, take a short break to immerse yourself in the music and the lyrics for more patience as you work.

Tilt Your Head Back and Look Up

This simple technique is a great way to soothe a busy, tense, or impatient mind. There's something about sending your gaze upward that naturally communicates to your brain that it's time to let go of whatever you're feeling so intently and relax.

Here's how to put this technique to good use:

1. When you're feeling an intense emotion and you want to calm it down, stop what you're doing and stand or sit still. Tilt your head gently up toward the ceiling or the sky. You should be looking upward, but keep it at an angle that's comfortable for your neck.
2. Let your eyes roll up toward your eyelids, bringing your eyebrows up your forehead as if you're surprised.
3. Simply rest here for a moment. If your mind wants to find something to look at, find a spot on the ceiling. If you're outside, find a cloud, a tree, or anything else that's overhead and stationary.
4. Stay here for at least thirty seconds, or until you find yourself feeling less intense and more patient.

Take a Downward Dog

One particular yoga move that can help build patience is Downward Dog. It's an inversion (a position where your head is below your heart), so it requires patience with yourself and your body to practice. It also provides a shake-up for your body and blood flow, which can give you a boost of energy and improve your ability to focus.

Follow these directions to give Downward Dog a try:

1. Roll out your yoga mat or a towel, or simply find a clear spot on the floor near you. Start with your legs folded underneath you, knees together, hands resting on your thighs.
2. Lean forward, putting your hands directly underneath your shoulders. Bring your hips up so they are directly over your knees. You are now in a "tabletop" position, and your back should be flat and parallel with the floor.
3. From here, curl your toes under and lift your knees, then bring your hips up high. You will be in an inverted "V" position, with your hands and the balls of your feet and your toes on the ground, and your hips and bum up toward the ceiling.
4. Focus on lifting your hips and pressing your chest toward your thighs. Try to keep your back straight, but feel free to bend your knees if that's more comfortable. Settle in here, and stay for a few deep breaths.

Allow whatever is causing you to feel impatient to simply melt away as you focus on the Downward Dog movement. If you're familiar with yoga practices, feel free to turn this move into a short yoga cycle, or find a video online to guide you through more yoga poses.

Picture a Peaceful Place

Visualization is a helpful tool to bring yourself to a state of calmness, allowing you to be more patient. Once you are able to neutralize any stressors while playing a calm scene in your head, you're more able to clear the way to patient thought patterns, both for yourself and whatever it is you're dealing with.

Find a comfortable seat and get cozy for this one. Here's what you do:

1. Close your eyes and take a few deep, calming breaths to get centered.
2. Now, think about what "peaceful" means to you. What feels peaceful? What elements contribute to you feeling at peace? Silence? Soft sounds? Still air or perhaps a breeze?
3. Imagine a place with these peaceful elements. Think about what this place looks like, what you might see around you. For example, you might imagine a quiet beach, the bank of a gently flowing river, or a serene forest meadow.
4. Imagine this place in detail. Sit in your peaceful place and soak in the feelings of calm, serenity, and joy. Allow yourself to become as still and patient as your peaceful place is.

✦

The secret of patience is to do something else in the meantime.

—REVEREND CROFT M. PENTZ
American author

Try Ujjayi Breathing

Calming your mind and releasing intense negative emotions is key to becoming a more patient person overall. This particular type of breathing, also known as "ocean breathing," is a fantastic technique for getting yourself in tune and finding a calm, neutral state of mind.

This is how ujjayi breathing works:

1. Get settled in and comfortable. Sit upright so you can breathe easily. Take a few deep, steady breaths to prepare yourself.
2. Create a small restriction at the back of the throat, making your inhale louder than normal. The "ocean breathing" nickname comes from the way this breath sounds—almost like a wave crashing on a beach.
3. Breathe in slowly, filling your lungs with air. Breathe out the same way, making your exhale sound like a beach (or Darth Vader, if you prefer that imagery). Continue breathing with this slight restriction for at least five breaths.

This focus on your breathing will help you feel more grounded, centered, and calm, opening a positive mental pathway for you to practice patience.

Stretch Up to the Sky

There's nothing like a nice, big stretch to shed some of your worries and feel more optimistic. Try full-body stretches to treat your body *and* your mind to some special treatment, as well as put yourself in a better state to practice patience. When you treat your body well, the mind often flourishes too, and vice versa.

1. Start standing up with your hands by your sides. Shake it out a bit if your muscles feel stiff or sore.
2. Slowly raise your arms out to a "T" shape with your palms facing forward, then continue bringing them all the way up over your head, rotating your palms to eventually face toward each other.
3. Once you reach the top, clasp your hands together and give them a squeeze. As you squeeze, lift yourself up onto your tippy toes and stretch your whole body upward toward your hands.
4. Hold this stretch for as long as your balance allows, then return to the starting position.
5. Repeat the stretch until you feel calmer and more present in your body.

You might scrunch up your forehead or make a silly face when you engage in the full-body stretch. Embrace it and lean into the funny face to bring some lightheartedness to your day. Just like when you're calm, it's easier to practice patience when you're happy!

Eat Something Sweet

Did you know the taste of something sweet can actually cause you to change your outlook, at least momentarily? Enjoy a sweet treat next time you need a reset on any impatient feelings that arise.

Research has shown that when participants eat something sweet, they are more likely to pay attention to romance-related words than the control group. People are even more likely to rate a potential romantic partner more positively when they taste something sweet!

Needless to say, feeling tense or impatient is an unpleasant experience, and you may even feel negatively toward yourself for feeling this way. When you eat something sweet, you are giving your brain a signal that says, "Hey, remember that sweet things exist? I deserve to enjoy them." Boost that signal by thinking positive thoughts while you eat your sweet treat, and you'll find yourself in a more positive, content, and peaceful state of mind, opening up your outlook to patience.

◆

Patience is bitter, but its fruit is sweet.

—ARISTOTLE
Greek philosopher

Drink Water Mindfully

Being mindful in general is a great way to practice being more patient: When you're grounded in the present moment, your thoughts can't drift away and focus on any annoyances you're feeling impatient about. Plus, it's always a good idea to drink some more water!

Combine the benefits of mindfulness and drinking water with this exercise:

1. Grab a glass or a bottle and fill it with water. Take a moment to simply observe the glass or bottle. Notice how the water looks in the container. See how it swirls as you move it.
2. Move it slowly to your mouth, but don't take a drink yet. Let it touch your lips. Feel the sensation of liquid resting against your lips for a moment or two.
3. Now, part your lips just slightly and take in a sip of water. Feel it sitting in your mouth, washing over your tongue. Swish it around your mouth, noting how it feels in each corner and crevice of your mouth.
4. Finally, swallow the mouthful of water and feel as it travels down your throat, through your esophagus, and into your stomach. Notice how it feels as it travels all the way through your body. Take a few more slow, mindful sips, taking short breaks in between.

This exercise will help you slow down, be patient, and appreciate the finer things—things as simple as drinking water!

Tap Your Forehead

It's not entirely clear how techniques like this one work to inspire calmness and patience, but the research shows that they do! Repetitive movements and somatic experiencing (i.e., involving your bodily sensations) help to ground you in the present moment, sharpen your focus, and get you in touch with your current emotional state. You might look silly, but give it a try and you might just feel more centered, less impatient, and better overall!

Here's what you do:

1. Find a solitary space to practice this technique. Close your eyes and take a deep breath in, then exhale it all out.
2. Take the middle finger of your dominant hand and bring it up to the center of your forehead. Gently tap your forehead in a steady rhythm of about one or two taps per second. Tap softly but firmly; you should feel it easily, but it shouldn't hurt!
3. As you tap, concentrate on quieting any tension, anxiety, or impatience in your mind. Focus on your goal: being more patient, right here in this moment.

Continue for a minute or two—or until you feel calm and present, and your impatience with whatever you are dealing with has dissipated.

✦

Patience is the art of concealing your impatience.

—GUY KAWASAKI

American businessman and early Apple employee

Shake It Off

Just like the title of a popular song by Taylor Swift, sometimes you can work through negative emotions and feelings of impatience by simply shaking it off!

Of course, you can't always "just shake" everything off—especially deeply rooted issues—but for everyday struggles that make you feel impatient, this mantra can work. If you're feeling irritable and impatient, give this technique a try!

1. First, find a private place to shake it off in peace. A dance floor also works if one is nearby and you're the sort of person who doesn't mind getting funny looks.
2. Make sure you have some space around you. You don't want to knock anything over or run into anyone!
3. Stand still for a moment with your hands by your side. Close your eyes if that helps, and focus on your impatience. Bring it to the front of your mind. Visualize it, dwell on it, put all your energy into it.
4. Once you feel like your impatience is nearly bursting out of you, shake it off—physically! Move your body as weirdly, erratically, or quickly as you need to in order to get rid of all that nervous, impatient emotional energy.

When you're finished shaking it off, take a moment to catch your breath and enjoy the release of the pent-up tension and impatience before moving on with your day.

Eat a Piece of Chocolate

To add another reason to eat chocolate, you can actually use it to be more patient. Chocolate is one of the few treats that feels like an indulgence and yet is somehow good for you.

Aside from the mood boost from eating something delicious, dark chocolate is high in antioxidants, and *moderate* consumption has been linked to reduced risk of stroke, lower cholesterol, lower blood pressure, reduced stress, and a healthier heart.

Also, eating chocolate mindfully can bring your awareness to the present moment and boost your sense of gratitude, making it difficult to feel impatient at the same time.

Given its many benefits, popping a piece of chocolate is a great, guilt-free way to take a break from anything that was making you feel impatient and indulge your sweet tooth.

Change Your Aura

If you're having trouble releasing unpleasant feelings of impatience with whatever you're dealing with, try changing your aura.

When spiritual people say "aura," they basically mean someone's energy. You can probably tell when someone is angry, ecstatic, or nervous, right? Often, people can pick up on others' auras without even interacting with them.

Here's how you can change your own aura:

1. Pause for a moment and close your eyes. Visualize your current aura. See it clearly, and note how it looks (e.g., color, opacity, shape, size).
2. Connect the way it looks to the hurried, impatient way you feel. Imagine what your aura would look like if you felt patient and unhurried. Visualize this calm, peaceful aura and note how it looks as well.
3. Change your aura to this new and improved aura. Watch as the old one fades away and is replaced by the new one.

If you don't believe in auras and think it's all a bunch of silly nonsense, don't worry! You can still benefit from this technique. It engages visualization and present-moment awareness to help you be more patient, no matter your personal views on the subject!

✦

Be patient. Everything comes to you in the right moment.

—ANONYMOUS

Personify Your Impatience

Personifying things can be a helpful way to work through your feelings, especially feelings of frustration or impatience. Personifying is thinking of something as an actual person. For instance, you might have personified your teddy bear as a child or maybe even your car as a teenager. If you imagine your impatience as an actual person, you are likely to meet them with greater understanding than you would normally.

Here's how to do it:

1. Close your eyes and imagine what your impatience would look like if it were a person. What features would it have? How tall would it be? What kind of expression would be on its face?
2. Give your impatience a name. It shouldn't be the name of someone you are close to, but don't pick a name of someone you dislike either. Try to pick a more neutral name, one that fits your impatience.
3. Now, watch your impatience as it shows its frustration. See it rage and storm around and throw up its hands in disbelief. Notice how silly and dramatic it looks. Address your impatience and tell it to chill! Say, "[Impatience], I'm not giving in to your tantrum right now. I'm choosing to be patient."

This practice might feel funny at first, but it's a great method of separating yourself from your more difficult feelings, and it helps you understand why you were impatient in the first place.

Role-Play a Patient Person

You don't always have to *be* the most patient person. Sometimes, you can make better choices by just *pretending* to be how you want to be. Eventually, if you spend enough time pretending to be the way you want to be, you'll find that you have actually become that person. This is what is meant by the popular phrase, "Fake it 'til you make it!"

So, if you want to become a more patient person, try role-playing a patient person. When you're feeling impatient, ask yourself:

- What would a patient person do in this situation?
- How would a patient person respond right now?
- How would this scenario play out if it was happening to a patient person?

Answer each of these questions in your head, and then decide to play the part! Act like you have been cast as the patient person in the play or movie of your life, and commit to doing the best job possible portraying this person.

Give Yourself a Hand Massage

When you're feeling impatient, it can be really helpful to treat yourself to something nice. While indulging in something else might not be *exactly* what you want in the moment—or even help with what you're currently feeling impatient about—it can still fill your "wants" meter a little bit by making it easier to tolerate not having what you *really* want. A hand massage is just such a luxury that you can treat yourself to, and you don't need money, special skills, or anyone else to do it.

Hand massages are a severely underappreciated luxury. When people think of massages, they don't generally think of hands. But hands are a great area to receive a massage! That's where you hold a ton of tension, especially in today's world of constant smartphone and laptop use. Think about how often you use your hands in your day-to-day life.

Here's how to treat yourself to a hand massage:

1. Start with your left hand. Flip it upside down, with the back of your hand resting on your leg. Hold your left hand with your right and gently press your right thumb into the center of your left palm. Move it in a circular motion.
2. Next, move your thumb away from the center of your palm, pressing firmly. Stroke up toward your fingers, down toward your wrist, and out toward the sides of your hand. After a few moments, switch hands and repeat the massage on your left hand.

This simple, easy exercise is a great way to create calm and invite patience into your day.

Enjoy the Breeze

When you take time to enjoy the *good* little things, you are better able to handle or shrug off the *bad* little things—and more often than not, feeling impatient is usually because of petty inconveniences! People tend to feel bursts of impatience about things that don't have a huge impact on life, like getting stuck in traffic on your way home or waiting in a long line.

If you're stuck in a situation like this and feeling impatient, try focusing your attention on enjoying one of the greatest little things: a breeze.

1. First off, find a breeze to enjoy! If you can't get outside right now, create a breeze by fanning yourself with a magazine, a piece of paper, or even just your hand.
2. Close your eyes and focus on the feeling of the breeze gently caressing your face. Notice how it feels as it travels over your forehead and across your cheeks. Take a moment to be grateful for the simple pleasure of a breeze.
3. Breathe in deeply, feeling your chest and shoulders rise with the breath, then let all your impatience go in one big, emptying exhale.

Play a Calming Scene in Your Mind

Visualization is a great tool for shifting your mind into a more patient state. You might be in the same place, but your brain doesn't know that! You can literally trick your brain into being calmer and more collected by convincing it that it's somewhere else, taking you out of your current impatient situation, and completely transporting you to a more positive—or at least more neutral—state.

Here's how to try it:

1. Close your eyes and take a few deep, calming breaths. Try to clear your mind of whatever it's stressing about right now, but don't worry if some of it sticks around.
2. Now, say the word "calm" in your head. Repeat it a few times.
3. Let a scene naturally play out in your mind with yourself at the center. For example, you might see a peaceful meadow and yourself seated underneath a tree, reading a book. Or you might see yourself wading through ocean waves with a beautiful, colorful sunset in the background.
4. Whatever you see, focus in on it. See it in as much detail as you can and immerse yourself in the scene. Allow the calmness of this visualization to seep into you, draining you of your impatience and irritation.

If you find that it's difficult to bring up something calm or to focus on it, practice this exercise a few times when you're feeling positive or neutral. That way, you'll be primed to go straight to the visualization when you're feeling tense or impatient.

✦

Trees that are slow to grow bear the best fruit.

—MOLIÈRE (JEAN-BAPTISTE POQUELIN)
French playwright

Brush Your Hair

Brushing your hair is one of those tasks that can make you feel impatient—especially if you happen to have knots in your hair, or you're having a hard time styling it the way you like. However, you can choose to brush your hair mindfully, with acceptance and patience for your hair, and remaining present for every brush stroke.

Here's how to brush your hair mindfully:

1. Find a brush and get into a comfortable seated or standing posture. Avoid the mirror this time.
2. Starting with the hair closest to your face on one side of your head, run the brush steadily through your hair. If you hit a tangle, work through it slowly and gently before continuing on.
3. Do a couple of passes of the brush on each section before moving on to the next. Work your way all around your head to the other side.
4. Notice how it feels to brush as you go. Pay attention to the feeling on your scalp, the feeling of the hair being gently tugged, and even the feeling of the brush in your hand.
5. Allow yourself to sink into the sensations and the repetitive motion, and let go of any stress or anxiety you might be carrying.

If you have very short hair or no hair, you can try the same action and think of it as a scalp stimulation instead of hair brushing. Use this exercise as a simple way to build up patience daily.

Water a Plant

Plants are great for making a place feel cozier and homier, and they help filter the air. You can turn caring for your plant (or plants) into a ritual, helping you build patience in your day-to-day life by caring for something and patiently waiting to see the results of your work in new buds, greener leaves, or even fruits or vegetables to harvest.

Follow these steps to use watering a plant to work on your patience:

1. Grab a watering can or a bottle and fill it up. As you walk to your plant, take a moment to pause and simply look at it first.
2. Observe the plant. Notice the height, the width, the shape of the leaves, and whether it has flowers or not. Notice the color and any discernible patterns. See if you can find holes, yellowing leaves, or drooping blooms.
3. As you water the plant, think about the miracle of growth. Consider how much your plant can do with a little bit of water and some sunlight. It's miraculous when you stop to think about it!
4. If it doesn't feel too silly, thank your plant for producing oxygen for you.

This exercise teaches you to slow down and it gives you a chance to do something mindfully and patiently. Plus, you'll enjoy the myriad mental health benefits of caring for plants, which is shown to alleviate stress and depression.

Ground Yourself in the Present

One of the best methods of neutralizing frustration and impatience is to put yourself firmly in the present moment. When you're in the present moment, you're not thinking about past mistakes or the frustration of waiting for something important, you're just living in the present.

Try this exercise to step away from your impatience:

1. Tune in to your current surroundings. No need to find a quiet spot or a comfortable seat—wherever you are is just fine!
2. Try to focus your attention on what is happening right in front of you. You don't have to look around or search for anything in particular, simply see what is in front of you.
3. Notice what you are hearing. Note whether you are smelling anything. Feel the sun, the breeze, the humidity, the chair beneath you, the ground under your feet, and anything else you are experiencing with your senses.
4. Stay completely present in what is happening around you for at least a minute or two. If your thoughts stray, gently bring them back to the present moment.

This tool is especially effective for impatience, because impatience is inherently a forward-focused state: When you think about what you want or hope to happen soon, you tend to ignore what's happening to you in the current moment.

✦

Patience is the calm acceptance that things can happen in a different order than the one you have in mind.

—DAVID G. ALLEN
Christian fiction author

Take Two Minutes to Tidy Up

If you need a quick way to diffuse impatience in a difficult moment, tidying up is a great way to keep your mind and hands busy. When you're anxious or frustrated about something, oftentimes if you don't find something to do with your hands, you end up using them in unproductive ways—like constantly picking up your phone to check in on whatever it is you're impatient about.

Try taking just two minutes to tidy up when you're feeling impatient.

- Find one thing in your immediate area that is not in the right place. Move it to an appropriate place.
- Find one dusty surface and wipe it down.
- Find one thing in your kitchen or bathroom that can be put in a drawer.
- Find one thing that can be thrown in the trash or recycling.

If you're a tidy person already, this exercise will resonate with you. If you're not, then it's doubly helpful—you'll get some organizing done and practice patience at the same time!

Pat Yourself on the Back

It may sound like a silly exercise, but patting yourself on the back can actually help inspire patience! You may find that you can often convince yourself of ideas you wouldn't normally hold when you *act* like you believe them. So, when you want to feel like you're capable of something that's difficult for you—like being patient—try giving yourself a nice pat on the back.

Here's what to do:

1. Sit down in a comfortable seat, but make sure you can reach your upper back.
2. Close your eyes, and say to yourself, "I'm having a hard time but I'm doing my best right now. I'm proud of how patient I'm being. Good job, self."
3. Open your eyes, reach your hand around and over your opposite shoulder, and give yourself a pat on the back. Offer yourself love for being patient.

If you're still holding on to that frustrated, impatient feeling, you will almost certainly feel like a fraud at first, but give it a minute. Building up confidence in yourself and your abilities will make it much easier to put things into practice.

Practice Deep Belly Breathing

Deep belly breathing is exactly what it sounds like: breathing from deep within your belly. It's a type of breathing technique that gets you in touch with your body and has a calming effect, making it perfect for practicing patience.

Here's what to do:

1. Find a place to sit where you can easily keep your back straight and your feet either on the ground or in a cross-legged position. Sit up straight to allow your belly room to move with each breath. Close your eyes and place one hand on your belly.
2. For a few breaths, don't change anything. Simply notice how it feels to breathe, and take note of how your stomach moves with each breath. Next, deepen your breath. Inhale slowly and fill your lungs, pushing your belly out with it. Pause for a moment then slowly exhale it all out, bringing your belly back in toward your spine.
3. As you take these big, deep breaths, use your hand to follow your belly in and out. Tune in to the breath and note how each one feels. Continue for at least ten breaths.

Focusing on your body will bring you into the present and get your mind off of whatever it was stressing about. Take advantage of this opportunity to practice patience while sending your mind and body some oxygen!

✦

Our patience will achieve more than our force.

—EDMUND BURKE
Irish statesman and philosopher

Do a 360-Degree Spin

As you know, mindfulness is a fantastic tool for dealing with impatience. Becoming aware of your surroundings and being present helps you stay out of your head, making it easier to work through frustrations and annoyances—those from earlier in your day or those coming up. Mindfulness also clears your head so that after practicing it, you may come back to whatever was making you impatient with a new perspective or solution that you couldn't think of before.

One way to get out of your head and firmly into the present is to take a good look around you. You can do that with the 360 spin! Here's how:

1. Find a place to stand with some space around you, preferably in the middle of the room or, if you're outside, away from walls so you can get a good view.
2. Moving slowly, start rotating. Take small steps and move smoothly. Keep your head in line with your body, looking in whatever direction your body is facing.
3. As you spin, really look around you. Take stock of what's there. Notice the details. Be firmly in the moment.

The spin should take at least twenty to thirty seconds to allow you to really see everything around you, so feel free to spin back in the other direction to double the exercise. Take a moment to sit down to dispel any dizziness. Be patient as you wait for your body to regain its balance and reflect on what you saw during this exercise, remaining grounded in the present moment for as long as you need.

Breathe in a Square

This breath technique is great for practicing patience with your body while also calming the mind. It's called "square" breathing because it devotes equal time to each of the four parts of breathing: the inhale, the pause after the inhale, the exhale, and the pause after the exhale.

Follow these instructions to give it a try:

1. Inhale deeply, counting to four while you breathe in.
2. With your lungs full, pause and hold your breath. Count to four.
3. Now release the air in your lungs, exhaling while you again count to four.
4. Finally, pause at the bottom of your exhale, counting to four.
5. Repeat this square breath ten times.

This quick and easy exercise is a perfect way to be more present in your body and to shed some frustration or irritation, allowing you to move on with your day with more patience. If you found it easy, you can challenge yourself to a square with five seconds on each side, or even six!

Do Thirty Seconds of Jumping Jacks

Sometimes, the best way to burn off your impatience or irritation is to get in some physical activity, and jumping jacks are a great way to do that. You probably haven't done any since middle school gym class, but why not dive back in? You'll expel some tension and feel like a kid again at the same time!

In case you forgot, here's how to do jumping jacks:

1. Start with your feet together and your hands by your sides.
2. In one swift motion, bend your knees slightly and jump, landing with your feet a couple of feet apart. As you jump, send your hands out to your sides and up, meeting overhead.
3. Jump back into your starting position and bring your hands back to your sides.

Challenge yourself to thirty seconds of jumping jacks, and you'll feel lighter and free of frustration at the end. If thirty seconds is easy for you, try sixty seconds or even two full minutes. As you catch your breath afterward, enjoy the pleasant, slightly tired feeling of physical activity, as you feel the stress and impatience from earlier fade away.

◆

The two hardest tests on the spiritual road are the patience to wait for the right moment and the courage not to be disappointed with what we encounter.

—PAULO COELHO
Brazilian lyricist and novelist

Kill Your Impatience with Kindness

Kindness isn't just for other people; it's also for yourself. Being kind to yourself is one of the best tools you have against impatience because when you accept your feelings as valid, you'll be able to work through them.

Here's how to use kindness against your impatience:

- Sit quietly for a moment and allow those feelings of impatience to bubble up. Let them exist; let them express themselves and be seen.
- Now, instead of pushing those feelings away or denying that they exist, offer them kindness instead. Meet them with love instead of hate.
- Pull up all the kindness you can muster, and direct it toward those feelings. Feel as the kindness rushes in like a river, surrounding, engulfing, and eventually drowning out the impatience completely.

When you offer yourself sincere and heartfelt kindness, you allow yourself to be authentically you. You'll meet yourself where you are, and say, "I am enough. I don't need to be perfect in order to be kind to myself; I deserve it, right here and now."

Meditate On Your Mood

Meditation is an excellent way to become calmer and more collected, especially when you find yourself becoming easily irritated and impatient, but can't put your finger on why. This is because meditation can bring up certain emotions or thoughts you've been suppressing, which is not always fun or easy, but is often necessary to help you process those feelings and get past them.

Use this meditation to pull out why you're finding yourself quick to impatience:

1. Sit in a quiet, comfortable spot and close your eyes. Take a few deep breaths to get calm and centered.
2. Now, focus on what you are feeling. See it in your mind's eye. Get a sense of what it is, and label the feeling (e.g., "frustration," "hurt"). Allow it to rise. Allow yourself to feel it. But while you feel it, start to dig deeper. As the difficult feeling is expressed, look behind it. Ask yourself where it is coming from. Follow it to its source.
3. Spend a few moments or a few minutes here, working your way toward the core of the feeling. When you feel like you have a good handle on it, start working your way back to the present moment.
4. Bring your awareness to your breath, then to your body. Finally, end the meditation with an expression of gratitude to yourself.

Based on what you find during this meditation, you can choose how to respond to your impatience moving forward.

✦

Only those who
have the patience
to do simple things
perfectly ever
acquire the skill to
do difficult things
easily.

—JAMES J. CORBETT
American world heavyweight boxing champion

Ask Yourself a Silly Question

A lighthearted, fun way to douse impatience on the spot is to ask yourself a silly question. Remember when you were a child and you asked the silliest questions imaginable? If you have a child or interact with children now, you know what this means—kids can ask the weirdest, most bizarre questions! These questions point to active and healthy imaginations. Kids are figuring things out in a novel and unfamiliar world, one question at a time.

So how can you use this to your advantage? You can copy kids and ask some silly questions in order to re-engage with your inner child, to feel young and curious and optimistic instead of set in your ways, frustrated with your current situation, or easily impatient. So, the next time you're feeling impatient, tense, let down, or just "meh," try asking yourself a silly question. Let your inner child out to play!

Here's some examples of silly questions you can ask yourself:

- What would my favorite color taste like?
- Why do we say "woof" to mimic dogs when their barks clearly don't sound like "woof"?
- Why is the moon called the moon?
- How are marshmallows made?
- What if humans still had tails?

Even better, ask a kid in your life these questions to surely get a giggle out of you both. Whether you can answer them or not, thinking about these questions for a bit will help you feel more lighthearted, and for a moment, might make you forget about whatever it was that was making you feel so impatient.

Do a Small Act of Kindness

Sometimes, the best way to quell your own impatience is to quell it for other people with a random act of kindness. If you notice someone else is stressed or worried about something coming up, a small random act of kindness is easy to do and can have a big impact on that person's life. Best of all, a small act of kindness doesn't just benefit the receiver; it leaves the giver with a more positive, more helpful, and kinder outlook too.

There are lots of reasons why being kind to others makes you happier and kinder yourself, but one important explanation is that when you adopt the kind of attitude or characteristic you want to see more of, you are living proof that it is possible. You know there can be more kindness, goodness, or compassion in the world when you are a bearer of it yourself.

So, in the interest of bringing more thoughtfulness, more light, and more happiness into the world, consider doing a small act of kindness. Here are some examples:

- Pay for the coffee of the person behind you in line if you notice they seem to be in a hurry.
- Make space in front of you for someone in a tricky spot during heavy traffic.
- Do a small chore around the house that you know your partner or family member hates doing.
- Pay someone a random, heartfelt compliment.

When you add kindness to the world, it's hard to feel tense, anxious, or impatient yourself. Use this to your advantage.

Do a Sneaky Ab Exercise

Exercise is a good way to get your mind off of worry and frustration and to force yourself to be more patient. Unfortunately, it's not always easy or feasible to stop, drop, and do twenty push-ups. Luckily there are some "sneaky" ways to take advantage of the benefits of a quick exercise!

If you hear "ab exercise," you probably think of sit-ups or crunches. But abdominals are one muscle group that you can actually exercise pretty covertly, even just sitting at your desk or standing around.

Here's how to do a sneaky ab exercise to focus your mind and practice patience:

1. While sitting or standing, flex your stomach muscles. Think of pulling them all in toward your belly button. However, try not to move any other muscles in your body.
2. Make them as tight as you can and hold for ten seconds.
3. Let go and rest for ten seconds.
4. Repeat six times, or until you realize you've let go of the impatience.

Not only will this exercise help you be more patient, it will also help you build up a strong core. It's a win-win situation!

Patience attracts happiness; it brings near that which is far.

—SWAHILI PROVERB

Fold and Unfold

While folding laundry mindfully is a great way to cultivate some patience, this exercise doesn't refer to laundry! Instead, it's about engaging your body in a different way: folding and unfolding yourself. Learning to move and relate to your body in a new way is a great method for dealing with frustrating or difficult feelings, like impatience.

Here's how to fold and unfold yourself:

1. Start standing with some space around you. It's a good idea to have a soft cushion or carpet underneath your feet. Breathe in and lift your arms outward. Take up space.
2. As you exhale, bring everything inward. Pull your arms in and wrap them around yourself. As you do, start to squat down. Bring your chin down to your chest, bend your knees, and bring your chest toward your knees.
3. Wrap your body into a tight little ball and give yourself a squeeze. As you exhale, stand back up, unfolding your limbs and reaching out, taking up space again.
4. Repeat this exercise a few times.

If you're pretty flexible, you can try adding in some kind of bind to get even more of a sensation of folding and unfolding (e.g., twisting, wrapping one arm behind your back, wrapping one leg around the other). As you catch your breath, feel the tension and impatience melt away, giving way to calmness and mindfulness.

Knead Some Play-Doh

Playing with Play-Doh is a great way to get out of your head and into the present, making it a great way to boost your patience. Play-Doh isn't generally something that adults interact with much—or, if they do, it's usually when they're following the construction orders of a toddler or scraping it out of carpet. But it's also extremely useful for taking your mind off of your impatience, keeping your hands busy, and taking some time to have fun.

Here's how to make it both fun and productive:

- Engage your imagination. Don't feel constrained to make anything in particular, just go with the flow.
- Don't worry about getting messy. You can always wash your hands and the play surface later.
- Use all of your senses (except for taste, of course). Smell it, feel it, see it, notice if it makes any funny squelching noises.
- Be mindful and attentive to what you are doing the entire time. Don't let your mind wander.

This exercise works well for cultivating more patience, because while adult matters may be stressing you out, forcing yourself to sit down, have fun, and be creative with Play-Doh is an act of patience in itself.

✦

The key to everything is patience. You get the chicken by hatching the egg, not by smashing it.

—ARNOLD H. GLASOW
American businessman

Color Something In

Coloring is a great way to invite patience into your life: It's soothing, calming, and it brings your heart rate down. It can also provide a way to express yourself and to engage your creative nature. Next time you find yourself impatiently waiting for something, try taking a quick coloring break to pass the time and find serenity in your day.

Don't have a coloring book? No worries! Try these alternatives:

- Doodle on a page and use your pen or pencil to produce different shading.
- Grab a piece of paper with words already on it and shade in the enclosed spaces of the letters. For instance, you can color in the big center of the "o" or the little half circle on a small "e."
- Color in logos, outlines, or anything else you can find in a nearby magazine or newspaper.

If you don't have any physical implements for coloring, use apps on your phone or computer to color virtually. Give yourself permission to spend a few minutes doing something fun and creative, and embrace the boost of patience as you focus on nothing else except your art.

Do a Simple Meditation

The meditation outlined in this exercise is simple, easy, and will only take a few minutes, but it will help you feel more centered and more patient.

While there are infinite ways to meditate, this is a great introduction to patience for beginners because it involves a simple direction for you to follow, veering from outside thoughts and worries, and simply focusing on the meditation itself.

Here's how to do a very simple meditation:

1. Sit comfortably with your feet on the ground or crossed underneath you. Close your eyes. Turn your attention toward your breath. Notice how it feels to breathe in and out. Follow each inhale and each exhale.
2. When your mind starts to wander, gently bring it back to the breath. Continue focusing on your breath and letting your thoughts go for several minutes.

That's it! That's all there is to it. You can set a timer for a few minutes or meditate for as long as what feels right for you. Remember to be kind and have patience for yourself when your mind starts to wander, which is totally normal.

Try Staccato Breathing

Most of the breathing exercises for patience in this book encourage you to breathe slowly and deeply. This is for good reason—it's the deep, slow breaths that ground you and connect you to your body and to the present. Usually, when your breathing is sharp and quick, it means you are on alert for danger, worried about the future, or feeling hurt or upset about something in the past.

However, breathing sharp and quick, or staccato breathing, can also be used for cultivating patience with attention and focus. You can use staccato breathing to feel more alert, alive, and present; just make sure you don't get lost in thoughts while you do it!

Here's how it works:

1. Start with a few normal, deep breaths to prepare yourself. Next, engage in a sharp inhale. Make a sound as you breathe in, quickly bringing air through your nose and into your lungs.
2. Now, with no pause in between, quickly exhale through your nose. Again, make a sound as you breathe out, and listen to the air rushing out.
3. Continue breathing in short, loud bursts, taking a couple of breaths each second. Focus on your breathing and the sensations you are experiencing as you breathe. After a minute or two, return to your normal breath.

You'll feel energized and ready to go after this exercise, but you'll also feel connected to your body and the present moment, allowing you to feel more balanced and patient too.

✦

No road is too
long to the man
who advances
deliberately and
without undue haste;
and no honors are
too distant for the
man who prepares
himself for them with
patience.

—JEAN DE LA BRUYÈRE
French philosopher

Do Some Mental Math

If you've ever had to do math in your head on the fly—perhaps for a retail job or as a server in a restaurant—you know it requires a moment of intense focus and patience. It's tough to concentrate on anything else when you're trying to multiply, divide, or parse out fractions without a calculator. You have to patiently shut out everything else surrounding you, and solve the math problem in your mind.

This is because your brain has to keep track of rapidly shifting information when you're calculating, so there isn't much bandwidth left for dealing with emotions.

Use this fact to your advantage when you're feeling impatient, and engage in some mental math! Here's what to do:

1. Look around you and find a number. If you can't find a number, quickly count something around you, like trees or cars.
2. Repeat the first step so you have two numbers in mind. Multiply the two numbers.
3. Enjoy the distraction!

If multiplying the numbers was too easy, try dividing one by the other, or doubling each and then multiplying the doubled values. Make it tough, and appreciate the patience it takes to solve mental math problems!

Challenge Yourself to a Thumb War

This is a great choice if you're waiting for something and need to pass the time or distract yourself from your impatience. You probably haven't waged a thumb war in a long time, which means that it's about time to try it again! And there's good news: You can't lose this one, because you're playing yourself.

Here's how to do it:

1. Sit with your knees slightly apart, elbows resting on your thighs.
2. Flip up your thumb on each hand, keeping your fingers curled inward. Place your hands together, knuckles pressing against each other and thumbs reaching toward one another.
3. Countdown from three, then begin the war! Try to outsmart one thumb with the other, wrestling for domination.
4. The thumb that pins down the other thumb for at least three seconds wins!

If this silly exercise doesn't distract you from your impatience, try making up new rules, like pretending you're the referee or the commentator, or adding trash talk between your thumbs.

Channel Your Kindfulness

If you've never heard of kindfulness before, using it for patience is a great way to learn about it! Kindfulness is where kindness and mindfulness meet, and it's a beautiful thing. Kindfulness is about being present and aware of your mental state and what is happening around you, while also approaching your experience with an attitude of kindness.

Here's how to cultivate and channel kindfulness for patience:

1. Find a seat somewhere comfortable and quiet, and close your eyes. Place your hands over your heart and let them gently rest there.
2. Pay attention to your breathing, feeling each breath as it enters and exits your lungs. With each breath, imagine that you are breathing in kindness, absorbing it into your lungs, and breathing kindness back out.
3. Let a soft smile come to your lips as you feel the kindness flowing in and out of you. Open your eyes and look around you through the lens of kindfulness. See the good in your immediate surroundings. If there is anyone nearby, smile at them and send them some of your kindfulness.
4. Let your hands fall from your heart and go on about your happy day.

Meeting any impatience you are experiencing with kindness and acceptance, plus an awareness of why you're feeling the way you are, is one of the best ways to remind yourself that peace is within your grasp.

✦

One minute of patience, ten years of peace.

—GREEK PROVERB

Cradle Your Face

When you're feeling impatient, self-love is probably the last thing on your mind. But it's also a great remedy for impatience as you meet any agitation and irritation you're experiencing with warm fuzzies—an excellent buffer against impatience.

Try practicing self-love by gently cradling your face to invoke feelings of being loved, cared for, accepted, and nurtured.

Here's how to do it:

1. Find a private and comfortable spot to try this one. Take a few deep, calming breaths to get centered first.
2. Reach your right hand up to your left cheek and cup it softly, with your thumb up by your eye and pinky finger down by your jawline.
3. Repeat step 2 with your left hand, so you now have both hands cradling your face. Use your thumbs to gently caress your cheeks. Run one of them over your lips if that feels good. Give yourself this soft, loving touch for at least a few moments.
4. Finish with a slight, affectionate squeeze of your cheeks with both hands, then let your hands drop.

Don't be surprised if this exercise brings up some feelings of vulnerability. Lean into them, and remind yourself that you deserve kind treatment, even—or especially—when you're feeling impatient!

Do a Body Scan

If you find yourself unable to stop thinking about whatever is making you impatient, a body scan is an effective way to get yourself out of your head. Follow the instructions here to give it a try:

1. Find a spot where you can lie down. Get comfortable with your legs out straight and your arms down by your sides, then close your eyes.
2. Take three slow, steady breaths, completing filling and then completely emptying your lungs. Turn your focus to your body. Starting at the top of your head, direct all of your attention to what you feel in that area.
3. Slowly move your awareness a little farther down, to about the level of your eyes, and notice what you feel here. Continue moving your awareness steadily down your body, noticing how you feel at each stage until you reach the bottom of your feet. Notice any and all physical sensations—an itch, a muscle spasm, a tickle, a bit of tension or tightness, etc.
4. Return to your breath for a few cleansing inhales and exhales, then gently open your eyes and get up and back to your day.

Once you've finished, think about what you noticed that you weren't aware of before this exercise. Note where you were holding the tension from your impatience in your body, and how you feel now. Also, pay attention to anything that feels nice and relaxed or at ease. Think about what adjustments you can make to feel more at peace with your body.

All men command patience, although few be willing to practice it.

—THOMAS À KEMPIS
German-Dutch monk

Practice Loving-Kindness Meditation

Loving-kindness meditation is the perfect antidote to the rushed, uncomfortable feelings associated with impatience. It's a specific type of meditation that focuses your attention on positive, life-affirming thoughts and feelings.

Here's how to try it:

1. Sit comfortably and close your eyes. Take a steady breath in and out. Bring to mind someone who you love and who loves you back. This person should be someone you feel close, comfortable, and relaxed with.

2. Imagine that this person is right in front of you, sending you their love and acceptance. You can feel it radiating through your body. Next, imagine that you are surrounded by more of this person, or others like this person who love and accept you. You can feel the love and belonging coming at you from all angles.

3. Now that you are filled with love and acceptance and belonging, send it outward. Direct it toward all the people that you love, all the people you like, all the people you *don't* like, and all people you haven't even met yet.

4. Once you have sent out that loving energy to all people, simply sit and bask in the glow for a few moments.

This type of meditation is excellent at driving out anger, frustration, and other intense negative feelings. Practice it to leave no room for impatience.

Create Blue Energy

Try using blue energy to inspire patience. People tend to think of blue as a soft, soothing, and calm color. It's the color of the beautiful sunny sky, the deep and ever-present oceans, and the serene rivers, lakes, and ponds that so often feature in your "happy places." You can use the power of blue to create and invite a sense of calm within yourself.

Here's how to harness the power of blue (or another color of your choice) to create calm:

1. Close your eyes and breathe in deeply. As you exhale, drop your shoulders down away from your ears.
2. Bring to mind the color blue. Notice what pops into your mind when you think about the color blue. You might associate the color blue with many things; if that's the case, make a conscious decision to focus on the more calming associations that come up.
3. Now, notice the energy that comes with these associations. It should feel soothing, gentle, and even serene. Grab onto that energy and apply it within yourself. Put it on like you would put on a coat.
4. Breathe in that calming energy, and breathe it out. Sit in it. Let it wash over you and through you. Absorb the gentle blue energy.

This exercise is a great way to induce a sense of serenity, which is often the antithesis of impatience. Try using this exercise whenever feelings of irritation and frustration bubble up for a boost of patience to your day.

Do a One-Minute Sprint

If you feel nervous, anxious energy due to impatience, try a purposeful one-minute sprint to relax your mind and body. Feel free to modify this exercise to a quick walk or jog. The important thing is to put some intense energy into a physical task for a minute.

Here's how to do a purposeful one-minute sprint:

1. First, make sure you're dressed for a quick sprint. You don't need to be in full runner's gear, but make sure you are wearing comfortable shoes that are appropriate for running.
2. Find a starting line. This could be a crack in the pavement, a curb, or even an imaginary line created by a stray leaf and a rock. Set a timer or check the time on your watch so you know when the minute is up.
3. Stand with one foot leading the other, knees bent slightly, gaze forward. Stare at a spot on the horizon and pour all of your anger, frustration, impatience, tension, stress, or any other negative feeling into your gaze. Focus it all outward at that spot.
4. On your mark (e.g., starting the timer, seeing a new minute start), take off! Run as fast as you can, keeping your gaze at that spot on the horizon. Feel your negative energy burning and falling off as you go.
5. When the minute is up, slow to a jog, then a walk, then a standstill. Think about how you feel. Do you feel slightly exhausted? Is your nervous energy spent? Do you feel more patient?

✦

Never make your
most important
decisions when
you are in your
worst moods. Wait.
Be patient. The
storm will pass. The
spring will come.

—ROBERT H. SCHULLER
American pastor and motivational speaker

What Would the Buddha Do?

The Buddha was a great teacher of patience, infusing the practice of patience into Buddhism's core beliefs. You don't need to be a practicing Buddhist to appreciate the Buddha and acknowledge his good ideas and positive teachings.

So even if you don't know much about him, when you're trying to be more patient, it can be a fun and interesting exercise to ask yourself, "What would the Buddha do?"

Try it now:

1. In a moment of frustration, pause and take a breath. Ask yourself, "If he were in this exact situation in this exact moment, what would the Buddha do?"
2. Come up with a response that makes sense given the almost superhuman patience the Buddha had. Perhaps the response is as simple as, "He would recognize how impatient he was being and smile at the silliness of his impatience," or "He would realize that his impatience was not going to help, and he would sit down and wait more patiently."
3. Whatever response you come up with, try to implement it!

It's okay if it's difficult to implement the response you came up with. The important thing is to realize that you have options, and that it's at least *possible* to act more patiently in the moment.

Use Your Body Breath

Your body breath is the breath that is created deep within and in loving conjunction with your body. Unconscious breathing tends to be disconnected from the body, mind, and spirit. Take some time to consciously and meaningfully connect your breath and your body to provide an excellent opportunity to practice patience.

Here's how to use your body breath:

1. Stand or sit up straight, so your abdomen is not constricted.
2. As you breathe in, allow your body to move naturally in response to the breath. You may feel your belly expand or shrink inward. Engage in whatever feels natural as you inhale.
3. As you exhale, continue to allow your body to respond however feels right. You may notice your belly retreating toward your spine, your shoulders dropping down, your chin tucking in toward your chest, your chest sinking, etc. Go with the flow.
4. Feel the connection with your body as you allow the breath to move you, and as you move *with* your breath. Continue body breathing for at least two minutes, staying fully present and engaged.

If this is your first time connecting your body and your breath in this way, you might note some exhilaration. That's totally normal! Be aware of whatever you feel, and be sure to draw upon those feelings of connectedness whenever you feel impatient.

✦

I take things as
they come and find
that patience and
persistence tend to
win out in the end.

—PAUL KANE
English writer

Challenge Your Perspective

When you feel impatient, you might start to sink into a negative perspective spiral. You might go from "Wow, this is taking forever!" to "Why does this always happen to me?" to "I swear, the universe is out to get me." This can happen fast, and it can be sneaky!

If you catch yourself adopting this negative perspective, try challenging it instead of allowing yourself to sink even deeper. Here's how:

1. Notice your negative perspective, and point it out to yourself. Identify it as a negative perspective. You may want to write down the thought. Note where the thought is false. For example, if your thought is, "I swear, the universe is out to get me," acknowledge that this is clearly untrue.
2. Provide some evidence to challenge the thought. You might list times when things have gone your way or when you've gotten really lucky. You could also note several of the things you are grateful for, which you surely wouldn't have if the universe were out to get you.
3. Review your evidence and remind yourself that you can choose to adopt a more positive and more realistic perspective. Note your new perspective. For example, you might phrase it as, "I'm dealing with an inconvenience right now, but everybody deals with inconveniences occasionally."

Sometimes, a simple change in perspective can help you rewrite your whole experience, making it easier to practice patience.

Channel a Patient Character

If you have trouble being patient, you might see yourself as being impatient overall. When you see yourself as an impatient person, it can be tough to work on becoming more patient. After all, if you truly believe you're an impatient person, what hope is there of changing? It's just who you are!

If you tend to write yourself off as an impatient person, don't lose hope! This exercise is a great way to challenge that belief and work on replacing it with a new one, one that allows you to grow.

Here's what to do:

1. Bring to mind a character in a book, play, TV show, or movie that you associate with patience. If you can't think of anyone, create a character who is a patient person. Spend a minute or two thinking about this character and how patient they are. Recall an example or two of a time when they were especially above and beyond patient.
2. Once you have this character and their patience firmly in your mind, decide to take on their persona. Step into this character and channel them. As this character, choose your next move. Decide how you'd like to act in the current situation in which you are feeling impatient. Do whatever they would do.
3. After you take whatever action they would take, see how you feel. Do you feel calmer, better, and more patient?

Remind yourself that you were able to be patient all along—you just needed motivation. Put the patient person role away for now, but keep it handy for next time you feel impatient.

Take a Sip

This is a simple technique for addressing any unpleasant, irritable, and agitated feelings, and inviting in patience. It's easy to do, you can do it pretty much anywhere, and all you need is something to drink!

This is how it works:

1. In a moment of frustration, irritation, or impatience, find something nearby to drink. It can be water, juice, tea, soda, or even a beer or glass of wine! It just needs to be something you can drink that you don't dislike.
2. Pick it up and look at it. Take note of how it looks—is it clear or more opaque? What color is it? Now bring it to your nose. Take a quick sniff, and notice how it smells. What notes are you getting from it?
3. Bring it to your lips, but don't open them yet. Let it rest against your lips, and notice how that feels. Part your lips slightly, allowing just a bit of the liquid into your mouth. Swirl it around, observing how it tastes and feels.
4. Swallow, and direct your awareness to follow it down your throat and into your stomach, noticing each accompanying sensation. Pause and savor the moment, then repeat with another small sip.

As previously mentioned, this exercise is simple—but it works! It forces you to be mindful and present of the physical sensations you are currently experiencing, which distracts you from your impatience. Repeat as necessary to work on being more patient in the moment.

◆

Patience is the art of hoping.

—LUC DE CLAPIERS

French writer

Give Your Sides a Stretch

Stretching is a great way to distract yourself momentarily. When you need more patience, get in touch with your body, and let go of the excess tension impatience is creating in your physical self.

People often stretch vertically, but when is the last time you stretched out your sides? Most people do a more "up and down" sort of stretch when they're tired, sore, or in need of some rejuvenation, but this type of stretch misses some vital areas on your sides.

Here's how to do a good side stretch:

1. Stand up straight and make sure you have some room around you. Lift your hands straight up above your head and start with a stretch upward.
2. Now, lean slightly over to the right. Make sure your head and neck stay facing the same direction as your body (in other words, make sure you don't twist to face the ground as you lean). Feel the stretch up your left side as you lean. Hold this position for a few seconds, even if it starts to get a little uncomfortable.
3. Repeat on the other side. As you stretch, make sure you're still breathing. Allow your tension to release with each exhale. Finish with another quick upward stretch, then continue on with your day.

Repeat this stretch every day or two to release any lingering tension and practice holding the position. Remember that it's much easier to practice patience when your body is comfortable and you aren't holding on to any stress physically.

Journal Your Impatience

Journaling is an excellent tool for meeting the goal of becoming more patient. It's helpful for staying motivated, for tracking your progress, and for working through any tough feelings or roadblocks that come up. As you work through any day-to-day impatience, you'll have a chance to write out experiences, and before long, you'll be able to flip back through your pages and see how far you've progressed.

Here's what to do:

1. Grab your journal and flip to a new page. At the top, write the date. Write "What's Happening:" then describe your current situation. What is so frustrating right now? What are you impatient for? Write at least a few sentences.

2. Next, write "Impatience Level:" and write down a number from one to ten signifying how impatient you are feeling right now, one being the least impatient and ten being crazy impatient.

3. Underneath that, write "Factors:" and note all the different factors that may be influencing your current state. You might write things like, "I didn't sleep well last night" and "I'm hungry."

4. Write "How to Move Forward:" and describe how you are going to handle your impatience. You might write, "Continue to wait patiently," "Go for a quick jog," or "Vent to a friend."

By the end of this journaling session, you should be feeling calmer. Your problem may not be solved, but you know what it is and what is contributing to it.

✦

Patience strengthens the spirit, sweetens the temper, stifles anger, extinguishes envy, subdues pride, bridles the tongue.

—GEORGE HORNE

English bishop and academic

Take a Mindful Walk

Mindfulness is a highly effective tool for battling impatience. The ability to stay grounded in the present moment, away from negative thoughts about things out of your control, is invaluable.

To work on being more patient in the moment, and to work toward becoming more patient in general, try taking mindful walks. Here's how they go:

1. Start walking! You don't need to set a particular time or destination. Feel free to wander. As you walk, ground yourself in the present by using all of your senses.

2. Look around you, and notice what you can see. Observe the people walking by, or the wind blowing the leaves off the trees, or see the dirt path in front of you. Engage your ears, taking note of what you can hear. Listen for the birds chirping, the cars honking, the dogs barking.

3. Notice what you can smell, like the crisp scent of a fall breeze or the smell of a nearby campfire. Notice how your feet feel as they fall on the pavement. Notice the muscles in your legs as you lift and place each step.

Walk mindfully for at least a few minutes to get the full effect. Just five minutes can replenish your patience for your current situation.

Visualize a Forest Getaway

When you want to create peace in a patience-testing situation, try visualizing a forest getaway. There's something inherent in forests that makes people feel safe, secure, and at ease. Perhaps it's due to the treetops providing a home for your early ancestors, along with things like shade, cover, and protection. Or perhaps it's the quiet and seeming stillness before your eyes notice the falling leaves and woodland creatures.

Whatever the reason people find forests calming, you can use this to your advantage:

1. Close your eyes and take a few calming breaths to center yourself. Imagine you are in a forest. The forest is made of tall, leafy trees, surrounding you on all sides.
2. Turn around slowly, and see all the greenery around you. Look down, and see that there are grasses, ferns, and other soft, mossy plants carpeting the ground beneath you.
3. Take a deep breath in through your nose, smelling the scents of pine and sap and clean, fresh air.
4. Exhale and relax completely, letting go of your frustration, anger, and stress. Remind yourself that nothing in the forest is in a hurry. The natural processes, including animals scavenging or hunting for food, require an innate patience unique to every living being.

Spend as much time in your forest getaway as you'd like, then come back to the present—just make sure to take that forest serenity and newfound patience with you!

Do Some Mental Time Travel

Instead of letting your mind hyper focus on your impatience, take control of the situation and choose to do some mental time travel.

Mental time travel is another way to describe thinking backward or forward to a different moment in time. Just as your thoughts drift off when you're bored, use the same technique to take your thoughts off of any irritation you may be experiencing over an annoying situation.

Here's how to set your course and mentally time travel:

1. Close your eyes and think of a moment in your life that you'd rather be in right now. This can be in the past or in the future. For example, you might choose a particular moment from a recent vacation, or you could choose a moment you think you'll encounter in a future vacation.

2. Once you choose a moment, focus all of your energy on this moment. What does this moment entail? What do you see, hear, feel, smell, think? Who is there? Set the scene for yourself in detail.

3. Now, hop in your mental time machine and you're off! See yourself transported to this exact moment in time. When you arrive, kick back and relax! Savor the moment you've chosen for at least a few minutes, letting your stress and tension melt away.

This is a great strategy for taking a break when you're feeling overwhelmed, agitated, or impatient. Come back to your current task afterward with a fresh outlook and remember that impatience is temporary.

With love and patience, nothing is impossible.

—DAISAKU IKEDA

Japanese Buddhist philosopher

Offer Yourself Compassion

When you're feeling frustrated, stuck, or impatient, it can be tough to remember to be kind to yourself, but it's so important! You are much more effective in making improvements when you approach them from a place of compassion rather than a place of judgment or shame.

Follow these steps to offer yourself some compassion:

1. Get into a comfortable seat and close your eyes. Make a quick mental list of the things you're struggling with right now. Don't worry about whether they're "big" things or not, just note as many as you can.
2. Consider how you would feel about a dear friend or family member who was struggling with this list of things. This should spark a bit of compassion. Take that spark of compassion and feed it. Gather up your caring, love, and kindness, and grow that sense of compassion.
3. Now, turn it around and send it toward yourself. Feel that sense of compassion wash over you, taking away your frustration.

This is a great practice to help in a moment when you've noticed yourself being impatient, but it can also be helpful to practice regularly for your overall mental health.

Offer Someone Else Compassion

The previous exercise (Offer Yourself Compassion) is a great way to fight impatience, but offering someone *else* compassion is also a wonderful way to introduce more patience! When you are feeling and expressing real, authentic compassion, there is little space left for any unpleasant and negative emotions, like impatience.

It's best to offer someone close to you compassion in real time, but that's not always feasible. Here are some of the ways you can offer someone else compassion in the moment:

- Call up a friend you know is struggling and ask them how they're doing—and really listen to their response.
- Text or email to a loved one who is struggling, letting them know you love them and you are there for them.
- Leave a heartfelt comment on a friend's social media post, sharing your love and compassion.
- Do a small act of kindness for a stranger, complete with a smile (e.g., holding the door for someone in a hurry, helping someone pick up something they dropped).

It's easy to offer kindness to others, and it brings you out of your own narrow experiences when you feel impatient.

◆

One of the
paradoxes of
life is that being
impatient often
makes it harder to
achieve something.
As with any skill,
you get better at
manifesting the
more you practice.

—SIMON FOSTER
Author of Manifesting Change

Dance Like No One's Watching

A carefree, lighthearted way to inspire patience when you feel annoyed and impatient is to dance like no one's watching. It's a popular sign to hang in bedrooms and living rooms, but few actually follow that suggestion. It's a scary thing—to dance like no one's watching! But it can also be incredibly liberating, helping you shed impatience and be more in the moment.

If you like the idea of dancing *like* no one's watching, but you want to actually dance *when* no one's watching, that's okay too. The idea is to feel free and authentic, and connected with your body for a few minutes, no matter who is (or isn't) around.

There is no one way to dance, and you should go with whatever feels right for you. However, if you're not sure where to begin, here are a few ways you can dance to ground yourself in the present:

- Try a popular, well-known dance that you enjoy, like the jitterbug, the Carlton, or the Dougie.
- Move your body in whatever way feels smooth. This might be swaying from side to side, taking small, light steps, or even slowly spinning in a circle.
- Lift your arms to the sky and sway them back and forth. Move your torso in the opposite direction of your arms, creating a "shimmy" through your body.
- Do a simple ballroom dancing move, stepping forward then backward in time with music.

There's no limit to the creativity you can apply when you dance like no one's watching. Go for it; allow yourself to live in the moment!

Experiment with a Mudra

Try using a mudra to help you work toward your goal of becoming more patient. A "mudra" is a term for one's hand positioning, often used in yoga and meditation. There are many different mudras you can try that involve holding your hand or hands in different ways, and they're all intended to invoke slightly different feelings, thoughts, or energies in your mind and body.

Any of the mudras can help you become more mindful, present, and patient. Take a look at the list and pick any mudra that feels right to you!

These are a few of your mudra options:

- **Gyan:** Touch your pointer finger to your thumb, leaving the other three fingers splayed out.
- **Buddhi:** Touch your pinky finger to your thumb, keeping your other fingers straight up and close together.
- **Surya:** Fold your ring finger underneath your thumb, leaving the other three fingers pointing upward.
- **Shoonya:** Hold your palm upward and fold your middle finger underneath your thumb, leaving your other fingers pointing out.
- **Apana:** Hold your palm facing up and touch your middle and ring fingers to your thumb, bending the other two fingers slightly upward.

Whichever mudra you choose, close your eyes and hold it for a minute or two, allowing patience in, and any remaining tension to move out of your body.

Challenge Yourself to Patience

If you have a competitive personality, this exercise may be especially effective for you to defeat impatience, so to speak. Sometimes, people have trouble motivating themselves or putting in the effort when they have nothing external to prove, win, or show for it. In these instances, it can be helpful to manufacture some competitiveness; you can do this by *challenging* yourself to be patient! Here's how to do it:

1. Grab your notebook or journal. If you don't have one, grab a piece of paper and a pen.
2. Write down what you're struggling to be patient with right now. Just a sentence will do. For example, you might write, "I am impatient to hear back from the doctor with my test results."
3. Underneath that, write out a challenge to yourself. The challenge should include what you are going to do and for how long. You might write, "I challenge you to sit in stillness for three minutes," or "I challenge you to relax your forehead and put on a gentle smile for one minute."
4. Complete your challenge!

If you need extra motivation, you can always start your challenge with "I bet you can't..." instead of "I challenge you to..." That way, you're engaging in some friendly competition between yourself and your impatience!

Take One Patient Minute

You can often "fool" yourself into being patient if you commit to even the smallest portion of time. That's why many people make a rule about going to the gym for just five minutes or getting on the treadmill for just one minute; they allow themselves to quit after that initial period if they want to, but they never do! It can be hard to get started, but once you do, you usually want to see it through.

Here's how to apply this helpful phenomenon to patience:

1. When you're feeling stressed and impatient, set aside one minute to be patient. No matter how busy or hurried you are, you can almost always find just one minute!
2. Tell yourself that during this minute, you will be patient. You will not be rushed, tense, or agitated—you will simply let go of all that and be patient.
3. Start a timer or coordinate with your phone or watch to begin. For this one minute, choose to be patient.

At the end of this minute, notice how you feel. Did it feel good to be patient during this time? Would you like to continue choosing patience?

Patience is a necessary ingredient of genius.

—BENJAMIN DISRAELI
Prime minister of the United Kingdom

Stop and Smell the Roses

There's nothing like your sense of smell to pull you out of a difficult situation that's making you feel impatient. Smell is the sense most closely tied to memories, and it can act as a powerful reminder of your past. Further, it has a strong but subtle impact on your mood and emotions. Use the power of smell to your advantage when you want to become more patient.

As you go about your day, take a minute or two to stop and smell the roses. Of course, you may not always have roses to smell, but that's not the point; you can stop and smell anything pleasant!

Here's a list of some of the things you may be able to stop and smell during your day:

- Scented soap
- A candle (lit or unlit)
- A piece of fresh fruit
- Something cooking (whether out on the town or at home)
- Your partner's or beloved friend's perfume, cologne, or other scented product
- Anything with a flower or blossom

What you smell isn't important, it's the *way* you smell that matters. Take time to be fully present and focus all of your attention on what you smell. Bring your mind back to the scent if it starts to wander. Practice being in the moment as you patiently take in the scents, and be at peace.

Surrender to the Present

Oftentimes, the things that make you the most impatient are entirely out of your control. Lean into this knowledge by surrendering to the present.

The idea of "surrendering" is a difficult one. People like to feel as though they're in complete control as often as possible. Learning to surrender not only helps you let go of this need to be in control, it also makes it *much* easier to practice patience. When you surrender to the whims of the present moment, you empower yourself to behave how you choose, regardless of any factors outside of your control.

Try these steps to practice surrendering to the present:

1. Come to stillness, whether you're sitting, standing, or lying down. Keep your eyes open but soften your gaze.
2. Breathe in slowly. As you do, commit to being fully present in this moment. Breathe out slowly. As you do, let go of any need to be in control.
3. As you begin to take another breath, realize that there is only this moment. The last one is already gone, and the next one has not arrived yet. This particular moment is the only one you will ever have.
4. Remind yourself that you are okay right here, right now. You have everything you need to survive this moment. You are perfectly capable of living this moment.

Repeat this exercise several times a day for more presence, mindfulness, and peace in your life.

Visualize a Still Pond

Use a visualization of a pond to bring yourself to stillness and cultivate patience. Still waters have the power to soothe and soften, helping you shed your tensions and worries, and be still yourself.

Here's how to do it:

1. Find a comfortable seat and close your eyes. Breathe in deeply and let it all out in a big exhale. Think about a pond. It's easiest to call to mind one you've already seen, so scan your memories for a pond.
2. Once you've settled on a pond, fix it in your mind. Bring as much detail to this pond as you can. See the water, the damp edges of the pond, the surrounding earth, and the grasses and plants that border it.
3. Imagine you are sitting in front of this pond. Breathe in the fresh air. Feel the gentle breeze on your face. Hear the soft sounds of birds singing or frogs ribbiting. See the still surface of the pond. Feel the calmness radiating off of the pond and absorb some of it. Let it sit within you, and allow it to grow.
4. Stay here for a few minutes as the stillness grows inside of you, then open your eyes and continue with your day, carrying it with you.

Spend as much time at the pond as you need, savoring the moment of patience and stillness in your day.

If we want to live wider
and deeper lives,
not just faster ones,
we have to practice
patience—patience
with ourselves, with
other people, and
with the big and small
circumstances of life
itself.

—M.J. RYAN
American bestselling author of the Random Acts of Kindness series

Be a Windmill

Tapping in to your inner child is a great way to cultivate patience. When you were a child, it's likely that none of the things that are making you currently feel impatient were relevant or even existed yet. This is a fun, easy exercise to embrace your sense of play, giving your body a good warm-up, and transport you back to your childhood away from your current feelings of impatience.

Here's what you do:

1. Stand up and make sure you have some space around you to stretch out your arms. Put your hands straight up in the air above your head, like you're surrendering to someone.
2. Begin to slowly move your arms in a circular motion, starting out moving toward your right, then down toward your feet, out toward your left, and then back up above your head.
3. Draw this big circle with your hands, but keep your body and your head pointing forward. Feel the stretch in your muscles as you move your arms.
4. After a few circles, reverse your direction, moving your hands toward your left side, then down to your right, and up above your head again. Notice the opposite muscles stretching with the reversed direction. Continue for another few circles.

If this exercise was easy for you, try upping the speed! Savor the moment of fun, and think back on other childhood games to try next time you feel impatient.

Wash Your Hands

Washing your hands is a great opportunity to practice patience, mindfully grounding your awareness in the present moment, and taking time to carefully clean your hands. It's something you do multiple times per day, but most people often do it mindlessly instead of mindfully. Try this exercise each time you wash your hands, and you'll find yourself becoming automatically more patient.

Follow these steps to give it a try:

1. As you walk to the sink, appraise the sink. See the color and the shine. Can you see your own reflection in the faucet?
2. Feel the smooth metal under your fingers as you twist the knob or pull the lever. Notice the feel of the soap pump on your fingertips, and note the pressure you use to dispense the soap. Feel the cool liquid or light foam of the soap on your other palm.
3. As you rub your hands together, focus on how it feels, how it looks, and how it smells. Can you tell what scent the soap is? Can you feel the soap washing away the dirt and grime of the day?
4. Enjoy the sensation of water flowing over your hands as you rinse off the soap, and feel the texture of the towel as you dry your hands.

Repeat this exercise each day for a more present, mindful, and patient you.

Cover Your Eyes

Greater awareness of the present moment is key to gaining patience; that's because your mind is not focused on past annoyances or future worries. One way to heighten your awareness is to deprive one sense to leave room for the others to kick into high gear.

Try this quick exercise to test the theory:

1. Sit somewhere comfortable and familiar, so you feel secure while you try this exercise. Set a timer for three minutes.
2. Take a quick look around you, then close your eyes and use your hands to cover your eyes. Make sure you can't see anything—no peeking!
3. Tune in to your body. Notice how it feels to have your hands resting gently over your eyes. Feel the seat beneath you and your feet on the floor.
4. Now, move your awareness to what you can hear. Notice each thing you can hear, and label it (e.g., "ceiling fan," "neighbor's dog barking").
5. Take a sniff and see if you can smell anything that you didn't smell before. Notice whether there is any taste left-over in your mouth from the last thing you ate or drank.
6. When the timer goes off, slowly lower your hands and look around you, continuing to patiently soak in the present moment. Take note of whether your other senses still feel heightened or if they've returned to normal.

Endurance is the crowning quality, and patience all the passion of great hearts.

—JAMES RUSSELL LOWELL
American poet, editor, and diplomat

Commit to Reducing Your Overthinking

Overthinking is the antithesis to patience, but it's also a self-reinforcing cycle that is incredibly hard to break out of. When you take the tiniest bit of information and stretch it out to a million different paths and possibilities, you open yourself up to worry and impatience for difficult scenarios that don't even exist. While thinking ahead and planning are undoubtedly helpful characteristics, there is such a thing as *too much thinking*.

Make a commitment to stop overthinking. If you want to be more patient and less fixated on your thoughts, try this:

1. Grab your journal or a notebook, and something to write with. Then find a nice quiet spot to sit for a few minutes.
2. At the top of the page, write the date. Next, write out this sentence: "I promise to work on reducing my over-thinking." Don't commit to *stop* overthinking completely, because that's impossible, but you can work on reducing the frequency.
3. Underneath this, write out a few things you can do the next time you catch yourself overthinking. For example, you might include going for a walk, reminding yourself to be kinder to yourself, or practicing a quick meditation.

That's it! Now you've made a commitment to yourself to patiently work on reducing your tendency to overthink. Remember to put it in practice the next time you start to get bogged down in your thoughts.

Scribble Out Your Frustration

When impatience starts getting the best of you, try scribbling out your frustration. Scribbling can be surprisingly therapeutic, even if the scribbles have absolutely no meaning. There's something about making your mark on the page that helps you release excess tension and blow off some steam. Kids know this—they do it all the time—but many adults have forgotten the healing power of the scribble!

Here's what to do:

1. Take out a piece of paper and a writing utensil. Close your eyes and take a deep breath in. As you breathe out, open your eyes and take pen to page. Start scribbling!
2. Don't worry about drawing a cohesive picture, picking the right words, or even making sense at all—just move your pen across the page in any way that feels right. Try watching as you scribble, then try looking away. See what feels best for you in this moment.
3. Continue for a minute or two, then bring your pen to a stop and lay it down. Take a look at the page and remind yourself that all of that mess is the impatience you just released. Doesn't it feel good?

Twist for Patience

Twists are a great way to reconnect with your body, give yourself a soothing stretch, and find some presence—all of which help you be more patient.

Here are a few different twists you can try:

- Lie on your back on the ground, and reach one knee up and over your body to the other side, keeping your shoulder blades on the ground. Hold for a few moments and repeat on the other side.
- While standing, twist your torso so you are facing to one side. As you twist, reach your hands down toward your waist, but slide one hand around to the middle of your back and the other to the middle of your abdomen. Repeat on the other side.
- While sitting, place your hands on your knees. Lean to the right side as you actively press your left hand into your left knee and bend your right elbow. Twist your head and chest toward the right. Repeat on the left side.

These are just a few twisty options; if you have another twist you prefer, go for it! Just make sure you're patient with your body, and take time before you untwist to fully feel the stretch.

To lose patience is to lose the battle.

—MAHATMA GANDHI

Indian activist and leader of the Indian Independence Movement

Sit in Silence

Sometimes, silence can be unsettling and make you feel impatient, so you resort to filling the silence or mindlessly scrolling through your phone. However, patiently sitting in silence can be incredibly restorative. In this exercise, you will greet silence as a friendly, comforting presence, helping you find the way to stillness and patience.

Here's how to boost your patience by sitting in silence:

1. Go to a spot that's as quiet as you can find. A bathroom, a cellar, or even a closet may be good choices.
2. Turn off anything that might be making sounds around you, like a fan or a humidifier. Turn your phone off or put it on silent—or even better, don't bring it at all—to ensure it doesn't disturb or tempt you.
3. Sit with your legs crossed or on the floor, and place your hands on your knees. Close your eyes and sink into the silence. Sit still and keep your breathing soft and quiet.
4. Focus your attention on the silence. Notice how it feels to be in such a quiet atmosphere. Soak in the silence and allow it to fill you with a sense of peace.

When you're ready to re-emerge, go slowly. Feel the difference in your mental state as you come back out to the noise, and reflect on how it felt to patiently sit in silence, waiting for nothing in particular.

Draw a Doodle

If you're finding it hard to concentrate, doodling may be the key to finding some patience. If you're an artist, you probably know the power of doodling; it can help you kill time, save you from the boredom of a long meeting, and keep your hands busy. What you may not know is that doodling can actually boost your attention and focus, opening the way to productivity and patience afterward.

Here's what to do:

1. Grab a piece of paper and a pen. Better yet, grab some colored pencils or crayons if you have them!
2. Sit down and get to work creating your own unique doodle. Use your creativity and go with whatever feels fun to you! You can choose what to draw, the size of the doodle, the colors you'll use, etc.
3. As you draw, focus on what you are doing. Notice the feel of the pen or pencil in your hand. Pay attention to how it feels when you drag your hand across the page. Note whether you can smell the ink in your pen or the lead in your pencil.
4. Try to absorb yourself in doodling for at least a couple of minutes. Once you finish your doodle, check in with yourself: Do you feel calmer and more collected?

When you focus 100 percent of your attention on the task at hand, you don't leave any brainpower for feeling bored, frustrated, or impatient.

✦

Two things define you: Your patience when you have nothing and your attitude when you have everything.

—GEORGE BERNARD SHAW
Irish playwright and political activist

Hum to Yourself

Humming a tune can simultaneously distract you from frustrations and remind you of happy memories, both of which can help you be more patient in the moment. Humming is a fun, easy, and totally accessible way to pass some time and add a dash of joy to your current experience.

If you're feeling frustrated and impatient, give humming a try. If you're not sure what to hum, here are some suggestions that you'll probably recognize:

- The graduation song ("Pomp and Circumstance")
- The wedding song ("Bridal March" or "Here Comes the Bride")
- "Happy Birthday to You"
- "Twinkle, Twinkle, Little Star"
- "Hey Jude" (by the Beatles)
- Your country's national anthem
- Your favorite song!

It's a simple task, but it can help! Give humming a try, and you'll likely find that you have more patience for tackling your current situation than you thought.

Move to a Different Room

One simple way to gain patience in your day is by simply moving to a different room. Moving out of a room signifies an end to whatever you were doing, and a fresh beginning for the next. It's like the feeling of relief when you leave work to head home, or the sense of calm when you enter your bedroom to sleep.

Apply this concept to leave your impatience behind while welcoming patience in—simply by moving into a different room.

Here's how to do it mindfully:

1. First, choose which room you're going to move to. Next, stand up and look around you. Take a good look at the room you're about to leave behind.
2. Walk slowly and purposefully toward your chosen room. As you walk, gather up the impatience, irritation, agitation, and any other negative feelings you're experiencing and prepare to let them go. Bring your hands up to your chest and imagine you're holding it all in your arms.
3. As you walk through the doorway to your chosen room, release your arms down by your sides and let go of all the bad feelings. Take a cleansing breath as you step into the room, then look around you. Notice whether the shift in scenery has done anything for your mood.

You may think emotions are more powerful and permanent than they actually are. Give a simple exercise like this a try, and you might be surprised at how much control you have over your impatience!

✦

If love is a sickness, patience is the remedy.

—AFRICAN PROVERB

Take a Quick Mental Nap

When your impatience is making you feel exhausted, and you're expending too much mental energy on worrying, take a quick mental nap. A mental nap isn't as restful for your body as a real nap, but it will give you a mental energy boost. And while it won't make the subject of your impatience disappear, you might get the mental boost you need to approach your situation with more patience.

Here's how you do it:

1. Find a comfortable space where you can sit down, recline, or lie down all the way. Set a timer for five minutes (or however long you have to devote to this exercise). Settle in and close your eyes.
2. Tell yourself that you've set aside this time to take a rest. You don't need to think about anything, remember anything, remind yourself of anything, or do any mental tasks. You have absolutely nothing to do but relax.
3. Now, put your brain into mental nap mode. Try to shut off those "urgent" functions that take so much energy. Turn off the worrying, the questioning yourself, the scheduling, and the planning ahead.
4. Spend a few quiet moments here. You can let your mind wander, dream, or simply sit still. Revel in the stillness.

The mental nap is a great way to enhance your presence, your focus, and your ability to be patient.

Tell Someone a Joke

When you're feeling impatient, there's nothing like laughter to take your mind off of your worries. Better yet, making someone else laugh is a natural happiness booster. You don't need to be a comedian for this exercise. The joke doesn't even need to be good! A "dad joke" is just as effective as a knee-slapper in this case.

The point of it is to engage you in the present, help you connect with someone, and lighten the mood. When you're feeling impatient, all three of these components can help you to enhance your ability to be patient.

So, press pause on your impatience, engage in the present, and lighten the mood with a joke. If there's no one nearby, phone a friend or a relative to listen to your corny joke. If you need some inspiration, here are a few excellent, horrible jokes:

- Why did the scarecrow win an award? Because he was outstanding in his field.
- You know the only mistake I've ever made? I bought an eraser once.
- Did I tell you about the time I went extreme camping? Yeah, it was *in tents*.
- Why don't eggs tell jokes? They'd crack each other up!

If these don't get the groan or chuckle you hoped for, you both can laugh at how bad the joke was itself! Regardless of your joke, try putting a smile on someone else's face for more patience in your day.

◆

Patience is the companion of wisdom.

—SAINT AUGUSTINE
Christian theologian, philosopher, and bishop

Write Something from Memory

One excellent method for distracting yourself in a moment of impatience is to write something down entirely from memory. When you engage your brain in a deep, memory-related task, you are essentially using all of your brainpower, leaving little energy to put toward being hasty or impatient.

Use this fact to your advantage and try writing something out from memory. It doesn't need to be perfect, it just needs to be close enough and to keep your attention for a few minutes.

Here's what you do:

1. Grab a pen and paper, or fire up your laptop or tablet. Sit down and think about a monologue, a song, a poem, or even a speech that you have memorized or nearly memorized.
2. Start writing! Try to write the entire thing down from memory.
3. If you get stuck and it's something you can find online, you can take a quick peek to help you continue on, but try not to look much of it up. Keep going until you've reached the end, and pat yourself on the back!

At the end of this exercise, you'll find that the intense effort has acted as a perfect distraction and channeled your energy into something other than feeling agitated or impatient.

Breathe Vertically

Vertical breathing is a great exercise to help you set aside your worries and practice patience. Vertical breathing is a practice that gives you a sense of lifting up and settling down. It's a soothing, repetitive activity that will help you focus and clear any negative feelings inside, clearing a path for positivity and patience.

Here's how to try vertical breathing:

1. Stand or sit up straight, making space for your breath to travel through your chest. Take a few normal breaths to settle in, then turn your attention to your torso, chest, and shoulders. For your next breath, prepare to think vertically.
2. As you breathe in, think downward: Fill your lungs all the way to the bottom. Let your belly expand outward, and you might even round your back a bit.
3. As you breathe out, think upward: stretch up toward the sky, creating a long, lean belly and looking slightly upward; however, make sure to keep your shoulders down and away from your ears.
4. Repeat this technique for at least ten breaths, then see how you feel.

This is the opposite direction to what you probably thought, and there's good reason for that: The typical way of puffing out your chest and lifting upward during an in-breath is actually not using the full capacity of your lungs. To practice patience, try different methods of breathing and see what works best for you.

Experiment with Feng Shui

If you find yourself feeling quick to impatience, you may have blocked energies in your room. Try switching up the energy flow with feng shui. Feng shui in your home is important because furniture placement can have a big impact on the flow of a room—and on your general state in said room. The energy flow can change a lot depending on how things are organized.

Don't worry if you don't know the "rules" or the "best way" to organize a room, because this exercise isn't about finding perfect alignment; it's about mixing things up, getting yourself moving, and thinking outside the box.

Start here:

1. Look around the room and find one "big" piece that you can move on your own.
2. Review the room and see if moving it anywhere else makes sense. If you can't, go back to step 1 and choose a different piece. Once you've found something, make the move!
3. Step back to admire your handiwork and decide if you can live with the change for a while! It's okay if you can't; you're free to change it right back if you'd like.

This simple act of moving things around and reorganizing—whether you leave it that way or not—activates your brain in a way that makes you see things in a new light. You can show your brain that change is possible, and these changes can benefit you. Use this new perspective to shift into a more patient mindset.

✦

When you encounter various trials, big or small, be full of joy. They're opportunities to learn patience.

—SCOTT CURRAN
Canadian author

Get a Little Silly

When you're feeling silly, you're in a state of mind so utterly care-free, that there's likely not a single thing you're impatient about. Try sparking that carefree attitude in a moment when your impatience is bothering you.

When was the last time you were silly, just for fun? Maybe you told a silly joke and got on a roll. Maybe you and a friend shared a laugh over a funny memory. Or maybe you reached that state of tiredness where *everything* becomes funny and you just can't stop laughing.

When we're being silly, we're in the moment, enjoying the moment. That makes it pretty much impossible to be tapping your foot, waiting for the next "thing" to happen. So, the next time you feel your patience slipping away, try getting a little silly!

Here are a few options:

- Play a silly (harmless) prank on someone close to you.
- Reminisce about a silly moment in your past with a loved one.
- Dance around like an idiot, no matter who is watching.
- Sing a song, badly—like, really badly.

Whatever you do, approach it with an air of supreme silliness, live in the moment, and let all your impatience disappear.

Do a Deep Belly Laugh

This patience exercise is a great follow-up to the exercise on the previous page (Get a Little Silly).

Laughing is a great activity for boosting your mood, putting you in a more connective state of mind, and even improving your physical health. On top of all these benefits, it can also help you move into a more *patient* state of mind. When you're giggling at a joke or laughing at some hilarious stand-up, you're fully present. You're not thinking about what you're waiting for, about what you have to prepare for tomorrow, or about what's on your to-do list; you're simply living in the moment.

Try the following methods to provoke a deep belly laugh:

- Talk to a friend about the funniest thing you can remember seeing or doing together. The more you reminisce, the easier it will be to put yourself in that situation, and the easier it will be to laugh.
- Look up your favorite silly video on *YouTube* or scroll the jokes on *Reddit* to find a good one.
- Put on a special from your favorite comedian, preferably one you haven't seen before.

If all else fails, you can try going for a deep belly laugh without anything to actually laugh *at*. Take a deep breath and force yourself to exhale it all in a big laugh that comes from deep within. Let it rock you, shake you, and reverberate through you. You may find that this flips the switch and it turns into real laughter! Before long, you'll forget all about whatever was making you feel impatient.

Try a Back Bend

Challenging yourself to try a backbend is a great way to work through impatience. You'll stretch out your body and mind as you channel your focus into the challenge of the present moment. Back bends force you into a slightly different perspective—and sometimes even a slightly difficult or uncomfortable position. As you focus on the back bend, you'll stop worrying about what's supposed to happen in the future. Plus, if you can't get your back to bend right away, you'll have to be patient as you practice it.

Here's a quick and easy back bend you can try to work on your patience:

1. Start by finding a chair or a counter that you can lean against or grasp if necessary. The portion you can grab should be at about the height of your waist or hips. Turn around so it's behind you, and gently rest your hands on it, fingers facing toward your body.
2. Putting some of your weight on your hands, begin to slowly bend backward. Keep your neck pretty straight, bending with your back instead. Keep going until you reach a point that feels uncomfortable, then stop. Now you can allow your neck to bend and your head to fall backward, looking up toward the sky or even behind you a bit.
3. Hold it here for a few moments, getting a good stretch up the front of your body and a good perspective shift.

Try this anytime you want to challenge yourself to be patient.

✦

A man must learn to endure that patiently which he cannot avoid conveniently.

—MICHEL DE MONTAIGNE
French philosopher

Create a Boundary for Yourself

Creating a boundary between yourself and your impatience is a great way to help you think around it. People tend to think of boundaries in terms of relationships with others, rather than as something they can put in place for themselves. But the truth is, boundaries can be helpful tools for dealing with anyone—including yourself. Boundaries are basically if-then statements that define how you will react when a certain situation arises, and you can apply them to your own behavior.

Here's how to create a boundary for yourself to help you work toward becoming more patient.

1. Grab a notebook and something to write with. At the top, write today's date. Next, write "My Boundary."
2. Think about a boundary you'd like to create to keep yourself accountable. For example, you might write, "When I start to get visibly impatient with someone, I will walk away and take time to cool off." Or, you might write, "If I'm feeling impatient and getting grumpy, I will set aside the issue and meditate for a few minutes."

Once you've set the boundary between yourself and your impatience, make sure you apply it!

✦

Patience,
persistence, and
perspiration make
an unbeatable
combination for
success.

—NAPOLEON HILL
American bestselling author

Offer Yourself Forgiveness

It can be easy to get down on yourself for being irritable, angry, or impatient, but that's just being human! Instead of getting bogged down about how you're feeling—and then maybe feeling bad about feeling bad—try offering yourself some forgiveness. When you're forgiving of yourself, you build your capacity to be forgiving with others too.

Here's how to cultivate some forgiveness for yourself:

1. Find a quiet spot to sit and think for a few minutes. Remind yourself that you're only human, and that all humans struggle with impatience.
2. Tell yourself that it's okay to feel irritated, impatient, and frustrated. That's a totally normal and totally valid way to feel. Acknowledge that everyone gets frustrated with themselves at times, and that you deserve to cut yourself a break.
3. Tell yourself, "I forgive you."

Take a moment or two to sit with your forgiveness, to really soak it in, and then go on with your day.

Offer Someone Else Forgiveness

Forgiving yourself for being impatient is a vital step toward self-love and self-improvement, but forgiving other people when they're impatient with you can also be an effective way to push yourself toward an attitude of patience and understanding. After spending time analyzing why you become impatient, it's hard to not be understanding of others when they feel impatient. And though it's hurtful when others take out their impatience on you, you can choose to end the cycle of impatience instead of continuing it.

Decide on who you'd like to offer forgiveness to in this moment, and make sure that you keep the following in mind:

- You can forgive this person by communicating with them (whether that's through face-to-face interaction, phone, text, etc.) or by simply offering them forgiveness in your own mind. You can choose the right method based on the situation.
- You don't need to get an apology in order to forgive; you can choose to forgive anyone at any time, whether they ask for it or not.
- If you offer someone forgiveness out loud, remember to be authentic with your words. Don't offer forgiveness for something you're not over yet, because this isn't true forgiveness.

After offering someone forgiveness, take a moment to check in with yourself. How are you feeling now? Do you feel more compassionate and patient?

◆

Patience and perseverance have a magical effect before which difficulties disappear and obstacles vanish.

—JOHN QUINCY ADAMS
American president

Have a Salty Snack

Contrary to popular belief, research has suggested that eating salty food can nudge you into a happier, more positive mood. And feeling happier and more positive makes it much easier to choose patience in tough moments.

While health experts definitely wouldn't recommend living on salty snacks, a little salt is okay! Don't stress about a little extra sodium now and then—unless your doctor tells you otherwise, of course.

You're welcome to go for any salty snack that calls to you, but here are some options on the healthier side:

- Beef jerky
- Popcorn
- Olives
- Cottage cheese
- Nuts
- Crackers
- Edamame
- Baked potato chips or other vegetable chips

To practice more patience, prepare and eat the snack slowly, savoring each delicious bite.

Break from Your Senses

Sometimes, when you're so focused on what's making you feel impatient, you can experience emotional "tunnel vision." This is when you can't think about or even experience anything else except your worry. When you're in the tunnel, you lose access to the skills, knowledge, and resources you've built up over time, and instead of carefully considering what to do next, you can find yourself reacting without thinking.

If you're feeling overwhelmed with impatience, try taking a break from your senses. Here's how:

1. Find a dark, private space where you can take a few minutes alone. If you're at home, your bedroom is probably the best spot.
2. Turn off anything and everything that makes light or sound. Turn off the overhead lights, lamps, fans, air conditioner, etc. Set your phone to silent or turn it off for a few minutes too. Sit or lie down in a comfortable position, then grab a jacket or a blanket and place it over your head.
3. You should have minimal information coming in through your senses right now. Lean into this sensory break and ignore anything that may filter through. Instead of focusing on what you're seeing, hearing, smelling, or tasting, focus on giving your brain a break.

You might find that taking this sensory break gets you sleepy. Welcome the rest, knowing that you've successfully dissolved your impatience.

Engage Your Senses Fully

Sometimes, you need a break from your senses to process your impatience appropriately, like in the previous exercise. But sometimes, engaging fully with your senses can help you become patient and present, and stay grounded!

If you're feeling overwhelmed by impatience, go for the sensory break. If you're feeling stuck in your head and irritated by impatience, try engaging your senses instead.

Here's how it works:

1. Pause wherever you are. Stop what you're doing for just a few moments. Ground yourself completely in the present moment by engaging each of your senses.
2. What do you see? Open your eyes wide, look around, and see everything around you. What do you hear? Pay attention to all the things filtering in through your ears. Notice as many sounds as you can, even the quietest ones.
3. What do you smell or taste? Take a big sniff and see if you can notice any particular scent. What do you feel? Do you feel your feet on the ground? Do you feel the fabric of your clothes against your skin? Pay attention to it.
4. Be completely present and engage all of your senses for a few moments.

At the end of this quick exercise, you should be feeling energetic, mindful, and patient, having experienced the present moment and moved your thoughts away from any worries.

✦

I have just three
things to teach:
simplicity, patience,
compassion. These
three are your
greatest treasures.

—LAO TZU
Chinese philosopher and founder of Taoism

Look at a Sentimental Photo

There's nothing better than engaging in nostalgia to pull you out of an impatient mood and give you some perspective. While many exercises in this book suggest remaining present, revisiting happy memories is a great reminder that impatience is temporary. You'll probably forget about your current situation sooner or later, but the memories in your sentimental photos will last a lifetime.

So grab a nearby photo that invokes some positive, gooey emotion in you and follow these steps:

1. Look at the picture for a few moments. Think back to when this photo was taken. Put yourself in this moment—even if you weren't actually there.
2. Remember or imagine what it was like in this moment. If it's a photo of you with a loved one, remember or imagine how great it felt to be together; if it's a photo of a beautiful spot, remember or imagine how it felt to be in that place, taking that photo.
3. Allow those positive feelings from the photo in. Soak in these positive feelings.

As you put the photo down and go on with your day, refer back to the warm, fuzzy feelings you got from the photo, especially when you feel impatience strike. Remember that you can always pull up these feelings if you need a boost!

Do a Slow Scan of the Room

Being present and mindful is a perfect antidote against impatience. After all, what is impatience if not being stuck in an intense longing for a future event?

When you choose to focus on the current moment and be present, you don't give impatience much of a chance.

One way to focus and be present is to turn your attention toward what's in your immediate surroundings. Here's how to do that:

1. Stop whatever you're doing and stand or sit still. Starting with the wall or corner closest to you, look toward it and start a slow scan of your environment.
2. Move slowly, taking everything in. Notice the lamp in the corner of the room, the chair that no one sits in, the papers or photos on the wall, etc.
3. Move mindfully, noticing each thing around you as you slowly spin in place. If it helps, you can label each thing as you notice it (e.g., "chair," "bookshelf," "plant").
4. Notice all the details you can, and use them to ground yourself firmly in the present. If feelings of impatience pop up, acknowledge them and gently put them to the side in order to focus on your task.

This slow scan of the room around you will help you get into the moment and away from whatever was making you feel impatient.

✦

Genius is nothing but a great aptitude for patience.

—GEORGES-LOUIS LECLERC DE BUFFON
French naturalist, mathematician, and cosmologist

Plan a Meal

Thinking about the delicious food you're going to prepare and enjoy later is a great remedy for impatience. By thinking about something you're looking forward to in the future, you're distracting from your impatience, while also rewarding yourself for practicing patience.

Here's how to plan out a meal:

1. Grab something to write with or your phone to take notes. First, choose which meal you're going to plan (e.g., breakfast, lunch, dinner) and when you're going to have it (e.g., today, tomorrow, next week).
2. Think about the foods you want to include in your meal and decide on the balance of macronutrients (e.g., carbs, fat, protein) and food groups (e.g., grains, meat, dairy products, vegetables).
3. Decide on a healthy, balanced meal to make and get planning! Look up a recipe for inspiration if you need it. Write down the ingredients you'll need and make a mental note to check the fridge and pantry to see if you need to go shopping.
4. Write down when you'll prepare and eat your meal.

At the end, give yourself a pat on the back for doing something good for yourself. When you nourish yourself (physically through the food and mentally by practicing patience!), you give yourself space to focus on self-improvement and self-development.

Watch the Clouds

When you need to slow down your impatience about something, try cloud watching. When you were a child, you probably watched clouds as a simple pastime. It's easy to sit and watch the clouds go by, and it's something you can do either alone or with a friend or loved one. It's also a fun way to engage your imagination and challenge your perspective. The slow movement of the clouds in the sky will calm your hasty mind and bring you peace and patience.

You may not have done any cloud watching in forever, but it's like riding a bike—you'll relax right into it! Here's what to do:

1. Find a soft, comfortable spot somewhere outside. Grass is preferable, but any relatively flat surface will do. Remember to grab a blanket if you're concerned about getting dirty. Lie back, put your hands underneath your head for support, and look up at the sky.
2. Find a cloud and focus in on it. Does it look like anything? Does it have a discernible shape to it? If not, think about how it might feel to touch. Does it look fluffy? If you can't find a cloud at the moment, no worries! Simply stare up at the vibrant blue sky and imagine what is behind it. Think about the clouds of gas out in space that look kind of like clouds.
3. Take at least a few minutes to continue watching the clouds.

When you're ready to get back to your day, notice how you feel. Do you feel calm and patient? Do you feel more creative and curious?

Visualize a Snowy Mountain

If you want to take your mind off of irritation, anger, or impatience, try visualizing a snowy mountaintop. Beaches and forests are common choices for visualization, and for good reason—they offer a great space to relax and unwind. But mountains can be just as peaceful and even more awe-inspiring.

Follow these steps:

1. Get comfortable, close your eyes, and lean back in your seat. Engage your mind's eye and imagine a beautiful, snow-covered mountain set against a clear, blue sky.
2. Build a detailed scene. See the imposing mass of the mountain jutting up out of the earth. See the snowy peaks contrasting against the blue of the sky. See the wind sweeping snow off the ground and swirling it around. Watch as the sun glints off the perfectly white blanket of snow.
3. Place yourself in the scene, perhaps at the top of the mountain. You get to look around and enjoy the beauty, but stay warm and cozy! Let yourself breathe in the peace and serenity of the mountain for a few moments. Then gently open your eyes and return to the present moment, but bring that sense of peace and serenity with you.

Remember to give yourself credit for practicing patience. Maybe you didn't physically climb all the way to the top of the mountain in your visualization, but you took the time to calmly work on patience, and that is an accomplishment as well.

✦

He surely is most in want of another's patience who has none of his own.

—JOHANN KASPAR LAVATER
Swiss poet, writer, and philosopher

Touch Something Textured

In a moment of frustration or impatience, you can bring yourself out of your head and into the present by engaging your sense of touch. It's an underappreciated sense, but even small touches can have a big impact.

Have you ever felt down or low until someone gave you an unexpected hug or friendly pat on the back? Even a brief instance of friendly or pleasant physical contact can give you a boost!

If you're struggling with impatience, try distracting yourself and getting present by touching something textured. As you touch it, send your awareness into your hands. Notice how it feels. Come up with words to describe how it feels.

Anything with an interesting texture will do! If you're not sure what to touch, here are some suggestions:

- A blanket (there are tons of options here based on what you have nearby: soft, nubby, woven, etc.)
- A yoga mat or exercise mat
- The trunk of a tree
- The leaf of a plant (particularly a bumpy succulent, like aloe or a cactus)
- The bottom of a shoe or slipper

Whatever you pick, pour your whole awareness into what it feels like to touch it. Once you truly commit to feeling the texture and nothing else, it will be impossible to remain grumpy and impatient!

Try Zen Meditation

Zen meditation is a type of meditation that involves releasing all thoughts—good or bad. While focusing on patience is a great tool for when something specific is frustrating you, sometimes focusing on nothing at all can spark a more patient perspective in general.

Here's how to practice Zen meditation:

1. First, find a quiet and comfortable spot to sit. Choose a cross-legged position that feels comfortable for you.
2. Once you've assumed the position, place your hands on your knees, palms up to the sky. Close your eyes and take a steady, deep breath.
3. Now, the hard part: just sit. Don't focus on anything in particular—even patience. Don't train your awareness on your breath, body, or an idea. Simply sit and allow your thoughts to come and go through your mind.
4. When thoughts do come up, stay objective and nonjudgmental. Do not assign value to them or shame, or congratulate yourself for any thought. Just acknowledge it and let it pass.
5. Continue for a few minutes, then gently come back to your surroundings. Open your eyes, take a few moments to ground yourself in the present, then stand up and go about your day.

Don't worry if this is tough at first; it will get easier and more natural with practice.

✦

When it comes to patience, we don't have to change old habits; we can build better ones.

—SUE BENDER
American New York Times *bestselling author*

Do Absolutely Nothing

When you're impatient, you might feel like you have to do everything to alleviate that feeling, even if the source of your impatience is entirely out of your control. To fight that impatient impulse in this exercise you'll do nothing. That's right, do absolutely nothing.

Even when you aren't feeling impatient, you might get too caught up in doing *things*. People tend to feel like they need to do *things*, all the time, or else they'll be bored. You may think that you need constant stimulation because that's largely how most people live their lives—but people don't actually need constant stimulation.

To give yourself a break from the constant "doing" and give yourself a chance to build some patience, try doing absolutely nothing for a bit. Here's how to do it:

1. Find a comfortable place to sit or stand for a few uninterrupted minutes. Set a timer for five minutes.
2. Do absolutely nothing. Don't read, don't sing, don't hum, don't fidget, don't meditate. Don't move, hop, or stretch. Do. Nothing.
3. Wait for the five minutes to be up.

You did it! Give yourself a pat on the back for doing what may be the hardest thing to do: absolutely nothing. If you felt uncomfortable, bored, or impatient for the exercise to end at any point during those five minutes, give yourself an extra pat on the back for continuing with it.

Be an Objective Observer

Being an objective observer isn't just for scientists and researchers; it's an impactful ability that you can cultivate in yourself to become a happier, healthier, and more patient individual. When you take on the role of objective observer, you let go of emotional attachments to what is going on around you. You shed the need to judge, opine, value, or reprimand. You take things as they come. You can see how this will lead to more patience: If you don't have any emotional attachment to what is happening around you, it's hard to feel anxious or impatient about things not going "your way" because you don't have a way!

Follow these steps to objectively observe:

1. During a busy or stressful moment—one where you don't necessarily need to do anything or interact with people—visualize flipping the "objective observer" switch.
2. Take on the role of the objective observer. This means to be aware and to see all that is happening around you, but to stay neutral on it. Think of a researcher in a lab coat watching the behavior of mice; she isn't emotionally attached to what's happening, she's simply observing and taking notes as objectively as possible. Be the researcher in your own current experience.
3. Continue observing for a few minutes or until you are called upon to actually contribute (e.g., someone asks you a question in a meeting).

This brief excursion as an objective observer will help you detach from what is happening around you and find peace and patience in a new role.

Play "Would You Rather"

If you find yourself feeling impatient and needing to pass some time, play a fun round of "Would You Rather." It's one of the many games you might have played as a child, but lost interest in as an adult. It's a game that's heavy on the silliness, curiosity, and creativity.

The rules are simple: Think of two scenarios that are at least somewhat related, and that each have pros and cons, then ask yourself (or a friend) which you would prefer.

Here are some examples, ranging from practical to outlandish:

- Would you rather have $1,000 a month for life, or $100,000 now?
- Would you rather have the superpower of flight or invisibility?
- Would you rather shake hands with a kangaroo or fist bump a monkey?
- Would you rather work as the official eyeball cleaner of an angry cyclops or the horn sharpener of a temperamental unicorn?

As you can see, you have a lot of room to be creative here! Come up with your own silly ideas, and you'll quickly find that you have more patience than you thought for whatever it is you're waiting for.

Patience is the remedy for every trouble.

—PLAUTUS
Roman playwright

Be Your Own Rock

If you're feeling overwhelmed, irritated, or impatient, now is a great time to work on being your own rock. The better you get at being there for yourself, the easier it will be to neutralize tough feelings like impatience and anger.

People often credit loved ones in their lives for being their "rock," or the steady, dependable presence they need to successfully navigate life's twists and turns. It's true, loved ones can be an incredible source of emotional support! But you might have overlooked that you can be your *own* rock sometimes.

Here's how to start being your own rock:

1. Imagine a beloved friend comes to you and tells you that they've been feeling impatient lately. Outline what you would say to this friend. Note how you would offer support, advice, or compassion to this dear friend.
2. Now, take all of that sweet support and turn it around on yourself! Tell yourself all of these kind things. Reassure yourself that you are there for you.

Taking the time to work on your patience is a great example of being there for yourself and being your own rock. It might feel awkward at first, but it will get easier with time. Keep at it.

Take a Rest

When you feel impatient to get something done, you may feel that rest and relaxation are a waste of time or that you could be using that time more productively. But rest is extremely important. It allows you to meet your task at 100 percent, rather than rushing through and leaving room for mistakes.

If you're waiting for permission to take a rest, here it is: You are allowed, and you deserve to rest. Here are a few ways you can take a real rest, giving your brain a chance to recharge:

- Stand in front of a window, in your yard, or in any scenic spot you can find, and simply look out at the beauty in front of you.
- Sit in a comfy chair with the TV, radio, phone, laptop, etc., all shut down. Just sit there for a few minutes and relax.
- Lie on your bed for a few minutes and relax.
- Get cozy and close your eyes for a few minutes, and maybe even take a real nap.

Choose whichever option feels most appealing to you and take a well-deserved rest. You'll feel renewed and recharged with the patience you need to take on your task when you're done!

◆

Our real blessings
often appear to
us in the shape of
pains, losses, and
disappointments; but
let us have patience
and we soon shall see
them in their proper
figures.

—JOSEPH ADDISON
English essayist, poet, playwright, and politician

Get Yourself a Gift

If you're struggling with being patient, try finding a small, meaningful gift for yourself that you can carry around. When you look at it, remember your goal to be more patient, and remember that you have love and confidence for yourself. It's best if it's a small gift you can take with you wherever you go, but you could also get something that lives in a place where you see it all the time (e.g., on your desk at work or at home).

Here are a few suggestions for small gifts you can use as a reminder to be patient:

- A framed photo of a beautiful place, a loved one, or both. Pets also count as loved ones!
- A small souvenir or trinket from a place you have visited and loved.
- An item or toy you can use to work out tension, like a stress ball or fidget spinner.
- Something with an interesting texture, like a particularly smooth rock.
- Something that took talent to make, like a small hand-carved figure or a homemade doll.

There are tons of options here, so feel free to pick something that speaks to you! If you can buy it from a friend or craftsman who inspires patience, that's even better.

Visualize a Peaceful Shore

Use the power of shores to boost your capacity for patience and find inner peace. There's something humans find incredibly peaceful and soothing about shores. It doesn't matter if it's an ocean, a lake, or a river; you can find solace and comfort in any water moving against a shore, whether it's gently lapping ripples or giant, crashing waves.

Follow these steps to build your visualization:

1. Sit down in a comfortable seat, somewhere you won't be interrupted for a few minutes. Close your eyes and take a few calming breaths to begin.
2. Now, focus your attention on creating a peaceful scene at the shore of a body of water. Whether you choose a roaring ocean at high tide or a babbling brook, take a few minutes to set the scene.
3. First focus on what you see. What does the shore look like? Is there dirt, sand, or rocks? Is the water more blue, more green, or clear? Is the sky sunny and bright, or dark and cloudy?
4. Once you have this scene set in your mind, take a few minutes to stand here and enjoy it. Look around you, and drink in the peace and the calm. Notice how the scene makes you feel, and embrace the positive state with open arms.

Once you come back to your day, make sure to bring some of that peace and serenity with you: It will help you to be more patient and understanding.

Try the 4-7-8 Breathing Method

This breathing exercise is a wonderful way to practice patience, as it both requires patience to perform and cultivates patience with its calming effects.

The 4-7-8 is a particular method of breathing that is well known for its soothing ability. It's a great option for people who are experiencing anxiety, going through a panic attack, or simply trying to quiet an impatient mind.

Here's how to do the 4-7-8 breathing method:

1. Make sure you're in a comfortable position for breathing (e.g., make sure your torso isn't compressed and you can fill your lungs entirely with air), whether that's standing, sitting, or lying down.
2. Start with a deep breath in, counting to four while you inhale. At four, hold your breath. Restart the count, and this time count up to seven.
3. When you reach seven, let go and exhale out all the air you've been holding. Restart the count again, and count up to eight while you exhale. Repeat this breath, starting again with the inhale. Continue for at least ten breaths.

If this exercise is tough at first, that's okay. It's a long time to hold your breath and to exhale! Try to remember that training your mind and your body to tolerate more discomfort and uncertainty will help you be more patient.

✦

He that has no patience has nothing at all.

—ITALIAN PROVERB

Dedicate Yourself to the Task

When you lose your patience, you may feel tense and uptight—both emotionally and physically. This keeps you stuck in the unpleasant and unhelpful mental state of impatience. It's hard to focus on your task when such situations arise, but that may be exactly what helps you the most.

If you're feeling impatient about something, try dedicating yourself to whatever task you are currently doing, or if you don't have something to do at the moment, choose a task to fully utilize all your effort.

Do these things to keep yourself on task:

- Tell yourself you're going to do the best job at this task that you have ever done.
- If you keep thinking about the cause of your impatience, remind yourself that whatever your issue or problem is, it will still be waiting for you when you're done. You don't need to think about it right now.
- Pay attention to how it feels to do the task; be mindful as you go about it (e.g., feeling your fingertips on the keyboard, your back against the chair, your feet on the floor).

This is not only a good distraction from impatience, it's a great way to get something done at the same time!

Alternate Your Breathing

Alternate nostril breathing is an excellent technique for boosting your patience. It's a common technique in yoga that helps the practitioner to relax, shed their anxiety, and find peace. Use it to calm your body, mind, and spirit in any moment of impatience.

This is how it works:

1. Start in a seated position with your hands in your lap. Take a few normal breaths to settle in. Raise your right hand up to your face and close your right nostril with your thumb. Breathe in through your left nostril.
2. Pause and hold your breath for a moment. During this pause, take your thumb away from your right nostril and place your right pinky finger on your left nostril, closing it completely.
3. Breathe out through your right nostril. Breathe in through your right nostril.
4. Pause, moving your pinky finger away from your left nostril and placing your thumb back on your right nostril. Repeat these steps ten times.

This exercise takes practice to get the hang of, but soon enough you'll be inhaling peace and exhaling impatience!

Be a Star

Try emulating the stars in the sky to add patience to your life. The stars you see in the sky have been patiently producing light and heat for eons. They're not in a hurry, and you don't need to be either! You can practice the patience of stars with nothing but your body. This exercise walks you through an empowering move you can use to feel calmer, more in control, and better able to overcome your impatience in difficult situations.

Here's how to be a star:

1. Find an area where you can stretch out and take up some space for this exercise.
2. Stand with your legs slightly wider than your shoulders. Take a deep breath in as you throw your arms out, making a "star" shape with your body.
3. Bring your arms back in and wrap them around yourself on your exhale. Repeat five times, breathing slowly and steadily.
4. On your fifth repetition, hold your arms out in the Star Pose and stay there for several breaths.

By the end of this exercise, you should be feeling calmer and more centered, giving you the power to choose patience over impatience. If you're still feeling frustrated or impatient at the end, try repeating the entire exercise or holding the pose for a few more breaths.

Channel a Crocodile

When you think of patient animals, a crocodile might not be first on your list. But crocodiles are incredibly patient when they are hunting, able to stay perfectly still for hours at a time to lure their prey into a sense of ease.

You can take a lesson from the incredible patience of crocodiles. Here's how to channel their patience:

1. Close your eyes and picture a crocodile.
2. See the crocodile almost completely submerged, in water up to its jaws. You can see its glossy black eyes peering out at its prey (not you, of course—you're just an observer).
3. Notice the complete and utter stillness radiating out of the crocodile. Tap in to that stillness, feel it in your bones. Decide to take on that stillness for yourself. Sit completely still for a few moments, channeling the crocodile's energy.
4. Open your eyes and get up and on with your day, but carry that calm, still energy with you.

Luckily, humans don't need to sit completely still for hours on end for food, but you can adopt and adapt that same energy from stillness and put it to use against impatience.

Float Like a Balloon

This fun and easy visualization will take you up and out of your current state of frustration and help you feel patient and light. When you feel impatient, you may feel physically heavy, tense, and coiled up. Finding a way to release that tension and feel light helps your brain make the switch from impatient to patient.

Here's how to do it:

1. Close your eyes and picture a balloon. See the balloon in detail: the shiny exterior, the long string attached to a weight, and the bright color against a clear blue sky.
2. As you watch, imagine the balloon's string is cut. It's now free to float. It starts drifting upward, bobbing gently in the breeze. Follow it as it floats higher and higher.
3. Breathe deeply as the balloon floats upward, feeling the breeze on your face and the lightness in your body. Watch it for a minute or two, then bring yourself back to the ground, keeping that sense of lightness with you.
4. Open your eyes and continue on with your day.

If you still feel dragged down by impatience, try following the balloon for another few minutes, and focus intently on the lightness as it floats.

Give a Sincere Apology

This is a great way to get yourself out of a negative state of mind if you're feeling guilty for letting impatience take over and affect someone else. If you have been short with or rude to someone while you were feeling impatient, or you've behaved in a way that doesn't align with your values due to your impatience, give this person a sincere apology.

Think about who you may want or need to apologize to, and settle on someone—just one person for this exercise, although you may want to eventually apologize to more people.

When you apologize, keep these features of a sincere apology in mind:

- A sincere apology is given with true remorse, not out of a sense of duty. If you don't mean it, don't say it.
- A sincere apology acknowledges that your actions were wrong, and notes where you went wrong.
- A sincere apology does not require forgiveness. Your apology target does not need to accept your apology or forgive you, although it's nice when they do!
- A sincere apology is for yourself as well; give it your all for your own sake.

After a sincere apology, you should feel lighter, more at peace, and more able to choose a positive path going forward. Plus, you'll remember the feeling so that you don't take out your impatience on others again.

✦

Let us not become weary in doing good, for at the proper time we will reap a harvest if we do not give up.

—HOLY BIBLE GALATIANS 6:9
(NEW INTERNATIONAL VERSION)

Clean Something Around You

If you're feeling nervous energy from impatience, try expending that energy by cleaning your home. Cleaning isn't most people's idea of fun, but it's a necessary part of being an adult. Since it's something necessary and decidedly not fun, it's a great task to do when you want to work on your patience. It will take your mind off of your impatience, give you something physical to do, and you'll get something productive done that you may have been putting off until later. Best of all, the end product is a clean environment that's more conducive to better mental health, peace, and patience.

You know your own environment, so go ahead and choose one small cleaning task that you can do right now. As you clean, focus all of your attention on the process. Notice what makes the item or surface dirty. Is it dirt? Dust? Food residue? Pet hair? Once it's clean, take a moment to admire it. See how much better it looks, and give yourself a pat on the back for it.

If you're at work or somewhere in a space that isn't "yours," consider it a small act of kindness for the space's owner as well as a patience booster for you!

Create a Safe Space

If you struggle with putting impatience aside, try allowing yourself to really feel the impatience before letting it go. People often repress or deny feelings that are uncomfortable, but the reality is that they will continue to resurface until you fully express them.

It can feel odd and uncomfortable to allow yourself to feel negative or difficult emotions when you're used to suppressing them, so here's a creative way to do it:

1. Close your eyes and relax into your seat.
2. Imagine a "safe space" that's customized for you. What does it look like? Is it an outdoor space or maybe a room? What's in the room? See it in detail.
3. Once you have a detailed image in mind, imagine yourself in this safe space. See yourself walking around, interacting with it.
4. Now, let loose your emotions! Watch yourself act out your frustration, stress, and impatience. See yourself responding how you'd *like* to respond if there were no consequences. You might throw things, break things, yell, and even punch things in this safe space.
5. Rage it out in this space until you're done, then watch yourself take a few deep breaths. Finally, pull yourself out of the visualization and open your eyes.

Keep this safe space in mind the next time you feel overwhelmed by impatience. It's a great place to get out some of that negative energy so you can come back to the present with a greater capacity for patience.

Make an Impatience Jar

Just as it's great to reward yourself for good behavior, it's possible to discipline yourself when you behave impatiently. Some people have a "swear jar" in order to encourage them to stop swearing. The rule is that each time they swear, they have to contribute money to the swear jar—a jar that they don't have access to or is earmarked for something they may not need personally, like a charitable donation. The idea behind this is simple—it hurts to lose money! People are averse to loss, and they're better at modulating their behavior if there are immediate negative consequences.

In this vein, you can set yourself up for more patient behavior by giving yourself a negative consequence to impatience. You can create a jar in the style of the swear jar, or you can keep note of the times impatience gets the better of you and round them up at the end of the day, week, or month. At certain intervals, take all the money in the jar and donate it!

Not sure when to contribute to the jar? Make behavior-based rules, like:

- When I sigh or roll my eyes at someone.
- When I snap at someone.
- When I use passive methods to make my frustration known (e.g., switching from one foot to another, looking angry) instead of verbally communicating it.

You know how you respond when you're feeling impatient, so come up with the best indicators for you.

✦

Patience is power.
Patience is not an
absence of action,
rather it is timing;
it waits on the right
time to act, for the
right principles and
in the right way.

—FULTON J. SHEEN
American bishop

Use a Loving Affirmation

Boosting your patience can come through self-disciplining impatient patterns and behaviors, but you can also practice patience through self-love and self-compassion. If you tend to beat yourself up about any self-perceived shortcomings, including your impatience, adding in some love might be the key!

Try creating and using your own loving affirmation. You can use this affirmation whenever you're feeling impatient, and especially when you notice that you're being too hard on yourself for it.

Here's a good self-loving patience affirmation you can use: "I'm a good person and I try my best to be patient. Sometimes it's hard, and that's okay. I choose to be patient and kind." Repeat this affirmation as many times as needed to go easier on yourself and encourage greater patience.

If this affirmation doesn't resonate with you, create your own! Just make sure it mentions patience and is kind and loving toward yourself.

Take a Forward Fold

Teach your body to be patient with the forward fold so that your mind can follow in turn. The forward fold is one of the simplest and yet most impactful moves your body can make. When you fold forward, you challenge your blood flow to work in the opposite direction, sending blood *down* to your head instead of up, and *up* to your heart instead of down. Just as you challenge your body to commit to this patience exercise, you're challenging your attitude to follow through, which is an act of patience itself!

Here's how to take a forward fold:

1. Find some space where you can stand and you have space out in front of you. Stand tall and raise your hands high above your head. Press your palms gently together.
2. Take a deep breath in, then exhale as you slowly fold forward, bending at the waist. Bring your head all the way to your legs if you can. You can bend your knees to make the stretch easier on your hamstrings. If you can't bring your head all the way to your legs, that's okay! Go as far as feels comfortable for you.
3. Stay here for a few breaths, letting your head grow heavy and feeling the stretch. Rise slowly, bringing your hands up and over your head as you stand tall once again.

This simple forward movement forces you to slow down and take a breath, and it soothes your nervous system—a surefire way to open the door for patience.

Flex Your Wings

This fun exercise can help you tone up your back and arm muscles, but more importantly, it will give you a sense of quiet control and a peaceful energy to counteract the nervous, agitated energy of impatience.

Here's how to flex your wings:

1. Stand up straight with your arms by your sides. As you breathe in, raise your hands out and up, bringing the palms together at the top.
2. As you exhale, allow your hands to slowly lower all the way to your heart. Hold your hands at your heart, palms pressing together, and pause for two seconds.
3. After the pause, take a big breath in as you send your arms out wide again, then bring them up to meet overhead. Repeat these steps for at least ten breaths.

While you complete this exercise, focus on making your inhales deep and steady, your exhales slow and steady, and find peace at each pause in between breaths. Practice this a few times a day to become a guru of patience in no time!

◆

Stay patient and trust your journey.

—ANONYMOUS

Connect to the Rhythm of Your Heart

Being more in tune with your own body means greater self-awareness, and a greater ability to focus inward instead of outward on factors that are causing you to be impatient. This exercise taps into this idea, helping you to feel more connected with yourself. Plus, as you focus on your heartbeat, think about your peaceful early existence in the womb to enhance your sense of patience and calmness.

You've probably heard phrases like, "Look into your heart," and "Your heart knows," right? There's a popular idea that some important and sacred personal truths are hidden within the heart. Tap in to your truest self that resides within your heart.

Here's how to connect to the rhythm of your heart:

1. Find a comfortable seat, lean back, and close your eyes. Place your hands over your heart. Press gently, just enough so you can feel your heartbeat.
2. Settle into this sensation, feeling it thrum gently in your chest. Sway to its rhythm if that feels right. Stay here for a few minutes, tuning in to your heartbeat. Slowly let your hands fall to your lap.
3. Open your eyes gently, keeping that rhythm with you as you return to the outside world.

Hold on to the calm, patient feeling that was within your heart as you move on with your day. Use this exercise whenever you need to tap in to some patience.

Appreciate the Beauty of Lights

When people feel impatient, they're usually not appreciating the things in their life, instead opting for irritation and taking certain aspects for granted. Turn your impatience on its head by appreciating some beautiful lights. This exercise is best practiced if you have a great view of twinkling lights, whether that's an energetic city, a buzzing little town, or the stars in the night sky. If you don't have any of these at your disposal, you can quickly find light displays to observe online.

Here's what to do:

1. Find the lights you'd like to use, whether that's right in front of you or on your phone or laptop.
2. Settle in and get comfortable, then train your focus on the lights. As you look, really notice the lights. See how brightly they shine. Notice whether the light emerges in one soft circle, or whether it shines out in sharp corners and edges. Is the light soft and gentle, or bright and energetic?
3. Think about how long it takes for the light to reach you from its source, and marvel at the speed with which light moves. Give a quick moment of gratitude for your ability to appreciate the lights.

It may seem like a silly exercise to look at lights, but you'll find that noticing and appreciating the ordinary in your life is a wonderful way to boost your capacity for positivity, mindfulness, and patience.

◆

Have patience. All things are difficult before they become easy.

—SAADI SHIRAZI
Persian poet and writer

Take a Break

When you're feeling impatient about completing a certain task, and not sure how to remedy it, there's one method that almost always works: Take a break! Breaks are not only for when you're physically tired or your mind is in a jumble; they're also for when you need to give yourself an attitude adjustment. Removing yourself from the situation—physically and mentally—is often the quickest and easiest method of containing and neutralizing your impatience.

If you're feeling overwhelmed by your impatience, give yourself a quick break. Make sure you:

- Remove yourself physically from whatever surroundings are causing you impatience.
- Focus your mind on something else, whether that's another task, sitting in stillness, or a fun distraction.
- If you're physically tired, rest your body during this time.
- If you're anxious or agitated, do something physical during this time.
- Take at least ten minutes to reset your brain and return refreshed.

When you come back, you'll find that you have more capacity for patience, and hopefully, more motivation too.

Practice Affirmations for Peace

Affirmations for peace can help you develop a range of habits that inspire patience, which makes them incredibly useful. When you create a well of inner peace for yourself, you are feeding a source of calm you can draw on in difficult moments. When you're at peace, you are able to see different perspectives and gain wisdom to see around impatience.

To start creating your own well of peace for patience, try repeating these affirmations to yourself:

- *I am filled with peace. I radiate patience. I am peace.*
- *I can find peace with patience wherever I am, wherever I go. I choose to find peace.*
- *Peace follows me wherever I go. I can always find patience.*

Choose whichever one resonates with you the most—or create your own—and repeat it at least a few times a day to dig your deep well of peace and patience.

Sit with Discomfort

Sitting with any discomfort is a challenging but rewarding practice in patience. It's one of the hardest things to learn how to do, especially in today's world of instant gratification and endless ways to make things more pleasurable; however, it's one of the most important life-changing skills you can develop for yourself. Sitting with discomfort reveals your resilience, your confidence, and your resolve to make the most out of any situation.

To start building this skill, all you have to do is allow yourself to feel uncomfortable and to simply sit with it. Here's how:

1. Notice when something is uncomfortable, but not life-threatening or about to cause serious injury (e.g., it's too warm, you have an itch, you hear a sentimental song that makes you sad).
2. Instead of immediately addressing the source of the discomfort, distracting yourself, or moving away from it, decide to sit with it. Feel the discomfort, whatever it is. Feel the heat, or the itch, or the sadness. Let yourself fully experience it for at least a few minutes.
3. After your few minutes are up, decide the most appropriate way to address the discomfort, and go down that path (e.g., getting up to turn the fan on, scratching the itch, putting on a happy song).

Addressing the discomfort after sitting with it for a while will make the relief feel *even better*. The more you can build up your tolerance for discomfort, the easier you will find it to be patient.

List Your Acts of Self-Kindness

Showing yourself gratitude invites peace and patience into your life. When you remind yourself that you are a person who was capable of all of your accomplishments, you'll realize that you are also capable of conquering your impatience.

Being able to give yourself a pat on the back (physically or metaphorically) is the beginning of true self-love and self-compassion, two vital ingredients for building up your patience. When you're grateful for yourself, you're far more likely to find gratitude for things happening around you, even if your circumstances are irritating or annoying.

Here's how to give yourself some gratitude:

1. Sit comfortably in a quiet, calm space.
2. In your head, make a quick list of some of the difficult things you've been dealing with lately. You may include something like stress at work or dealing with a loved one's health issue.
3. Now, make another list with some of the good things you've done for yourself lately. You might include things like exercising, saving money, or reading a self-help book.
4. Imagine that someone you love very much did those good things for you—they exercised for you, saved money for you, or read a self-help book for you somehow.
5. Take that feeling of gratitude that arises and send it toward yourself. Thank yourself for doing something good for you, just as you would thank a loved one for a favor.

Learning to thank yourself for the good things you do for *you* is key to becoming kinder, calmer, and more patient.

Patience and fortitude conquer all things.

—RALPH WALDO EMERSON

American essayist, lecturer, philosopher, and poet

Hit the Pause Button

If you want to build up your capacity for patience, find the "pause button"! Not an actual pause button on a remote, but the imaginary pause button in your brain. When you practice pausing and observing instead of immediately reacting, you set yourself up for patience. You effectively stop yourself from acting out in a way that you might regret later, and give yourself time to process your impatience.

Here's how to hit the pause button:

1. Notice when you're feeling emotionally overwhelmed or agitated. Visualize yourself hitting a big, shiny pause button on your emotional state.
2. When you hit the button, all emotions and mental states immediately freeze. In other words, you don't spiral into a worse place, but you don't feel better either—you simply pause it.
3. Now, you have some time to observe. Take note of what you're feeling, and think about why you're feeling the way you feel. You can use this time to reflect, to journal, to meditate, or to do anything else that might help you understand yourself a bit better or help you deal with your current situation.
4. When you're ready to go back and address it, or leave it behind, visualize hitting the same button to "un-pause" your emotional state.

It might sound difficult at first, but with practice, you'll find it easier and easier to hit the metaphorical pause button on impatience.

Think Before Responding

When you practice thinking before you respond to emotion-spiking scenarios, you create a deep reserve of patience that you can draw on when things get tough. You might feel like your emotions drive your behavior, but you have emotions *and* a thinking mind for a reason: When your heart and brain work in harmony, you can create your best life.

Follow these instructions to think before you respond:

1. As soon as you realize that something has got your emotions up, remind yourself to pause (the exercise on the previous page can help you with this).
2. Instead of reacting immediately, set yourself a time limit. The amount of time will depend on the situation, but consider setting a time limit of at least ten seconds before you do or say anything.
3. During your allotted time, think deeply about the situation you're in and about what would improve the situation. Ask yourself if your instinctive reaction (e.g., yelling, saying something mean) would actually help. If it wouldn't, ask yourself what opposite action might help (e.g., speaking softly, saying something constructive).

Thinking before you respond is a skill that absolutely requires practice, but one that will benefit you in nearly all sticky situations with another person. You'll build your patience each time you practice it.

Practice Audible Breathing

When you tune in to your breath, you automatically become more centered, more focused, and better able to handle difficult situations. It's almost a "cheat code" for becoming more patient in the moment.

You might feel like you should make *less* noise while going about your daily business and not more, but in this exercise, you're going to fight that impulse and make *more* noise.

Here are the very simple instructions to practicing audible breathing:

- On your inhale, breathe in through your nose and make it loud! Exaggerate the action of breathing in so you can hear the air as it enters your nostrils.
- As you exhale, breathe out through your nose, and make some noise again.
- Don't rush your breath in order to make noise (sucking in air and pushing it out quickly); instead, try to make it steady and loud.

Practice breathing this way for a couple minutes at a time, focusing on how it feels. When you feel impatient or frustrated, pull out this technique for some instant calm.

✦

Being a good
teacher takes
patience; being a
good doctor also
takes patience. In
fact, if you want to
excel in anything,
master any skill,
patience is an asset.

—EKNATH EASWARAN
*Indian spiritual teacher, author, and translator
and interpreter of religious texts*

Label Thoughts and Sensations

When in doubt about how to best respond to a situation that's making you feel impatient, but you're not sure why, try labeling all your thoughts and emotions. There is tremendous power in simply labeling what you are experiencing. This simple technique will help you identify and categorize what you're going through, and you can then use what you've discovered to determine how to best respond.

Here's how to put labeling to work for you:

1. Sit quietly with your eyes closed. Take a few breaths to center yourself, then visualize two boxes in your mind: one that says "Thoughts" and the other that says "Feelings."
2. Now, direct your energy toward stillness. Of course, thoughts and feelings will arise when you direct yourself to be still. That's human nature.
3. When they do arise, notice them. Take them one at a time. Determine whether it's a thought (i.e., thoughts, emotions, images, etc.) or a feeling (i.e., a physical sensation) that you're experiencing, and imagine putting it in the appropriate box.
4. Continue labeling and organizing your thoughts and feelings for a few minutes. Return to your breath, taking a few steady and aware breaths before opening your eyes and getting back to your day.

The simple act of labeling will allow you to understand your thoughts and feelings, help you learn how to cope and respond to your situation, and build your capacity for patience.

Take a Wide-Legged Forward Fold

This version of the forward fold takes up more space and involves more use of your core, which can help you build inner strength and the confidence you need to choose patience.

Here's how to try it:

1. Stand up straight in the middle of the room you're in, or anywhere with some space to move around.
2. Scoot your feet out so that your stance is a wide one, with your feet at least a foot or so out past shoulder width. Your eye level should be a few inches lower than before.
3. Put your hands on your hips and start to slowly bend forward at the waist, but keep your back straight. Pretend you are standing at the edge of a pond and peering over it to see your reflection.
4. Continue until you get to the point where it's too difficult to keep a straight back. At this point, relax into the fold and allow your head to hang heavily toward the ground. Stay in this position, with your hands on the ground beneath you or on your ankles, for at least thirty seconds.
5. Finally, lift your hands back to your hips and slowly reverse direction, coming back to a flat back and slowly rising up to a standing position.

This simple exercise will challenge you to take a new perspective on something you might have already been familiar with, which is a lesson you can apply to patience as well. You'll also build inner strength, mentally and physically, to tackle any impatience that might arise during your day.

Try Patience-Focused Squats

If physical exertion gets your mind off of outside factors and onto yourself, exercising is a great option for practicing patience. It provides a double benefit: It distracts you from thinking about your impatience, while also building your physical *and* mental strength. That mental strength can help you with your discipline and self-control, two skills you can utilize to choose patience more readily in tough situations.

Here's how to do some mindful, patience-focused squats:

1. Find some space in the room you're in, or head outside to shake things up. Position your feet slightly wider than shoulder-width apart, toes pointing directly forward. Hold your hands up in front of your chest in loose fists.
2. As you begin, squat down as far as you comfortably can while keeping your toes in view (i.e., keeping your knees from going out over your toes).
3. At the bottom of your squat, hold for just a moment while you say the word "patience" to yourself, either in your head or out loud.
4. Rise steadily back to a standing position. Repeat as many times as you can before your muscles start to shake or you're too tired to go on.

Doing any form of strength-training can help you build patience with yourself, but doing patience-focused squats are especially physically challenging, so they're a perfect exercise for mastering patience.

✦

Patience is when you're supposed to be mad but you choose to understand.

—ANONYMOUS

Come Into Now

When you fully accept the current moment, you learn how to be completely in the now, severing all ties to impatience.

You spend your entire life in the present. Think about it—not a single moment of your life was ever experienced as "the past" or "the future," it all happened in your "now." Just as this current moment is happening in the now. This may be a funny concept to wrap your head around, but once you do, you can create a fantastic way to step away from anxiety and discover how to stop ruminating, worrying, and dwelling on impatience.

Here's how to do it:

1. Stop whatever you're doing at the moment and take a pause. Recognize that you are living your life *right now*, and that this moment is really all you have ever had or will ever have.
2. Look around you, and drink in what it's like to be alive right here, right now.
3. Feel the rising sense of gratitude for the present. Allow it to infuse you, to radiate out of you.

When you are firmly rooted in the now, there is no room left to be impatient about the future; there is only the now, and a deep, meaningful sense of appreciation for it.

Find Some Connection

One of the best ways to bring yourself out of an impatient mood is to make a genuine connection with someone. When you're appreciating a connection, you're too busy to notice that your desired outcome is not arriving, happening, or unfolding as quickly as you'd like.

To take advantage of this helpful human hack, all you need to do is reach out. Here are a few ways to do it:

- Reach out to a loved one through calling or messaging. You can check in, share news from your day, ask about their day, share a meme, or do anything else to get that feeling of connection.
- Get to know the person or people you are with better. Whether it's your coworkers, acquaintances, or friends, try asking some questions and listening to their responses.
- Connect with a complete stranger. Find something you have in common based on how they're dressed or what they're doing, and start a friendly chat.

This method works nearly 100 percent of the time, as long as you are open to keep trying until you make a connection. Your impatience won't be able to survive because you're enjoying a brief but meaningful moment of connection with someone.

◆

The keys to patience are acceptance and faith. Accept things as they are, and look realistically at the world around you. Have faith in yourself and in the direction you have chosen.

—RALPH MARSTON
Creator of The Daily Motivator *blog*

Visualize Soothing Yourself

You can provide a soothing touch to help yourself feel calmer, more relaxed, and more patient. When you were little and you needed some reassurance, what did your parent or caregiver do for you? They likely did a few things, including speaking soothingly to you, or even talking you through solving it yourself, but they probably also did a universally reassuring act: hold you close.

It's wired in your DNA to be soothed and calmed by being held by someone who loves you. It's why babies crave so much physical attention and why skin-to-skin contact is so vital for bonding. It's great to get this sort of reassurance from others, but you might have forgotten that you can give yourself this same type of reassurance. Next time you're feeling physically wound up because of impatience, try holding yourself close.

Here are the simple instructions:

1. Get into a comfortable position, whether that's standing, sitting, or lying down. Wrap your arms around yourself in a way that feels soothing to you and curl inward. You might end up in a fetal position if that feels right.
2. As you do, visualize holding a very small version of yourself in your hands. Cradle this "mini-you" and hold them close, soothing their worries away.
3. Continue for a few minutes, or until your frustration or agitation is washed away.

Once you figure out how to soothe yourself, you'll have access to on-demand comfort and patience!

Breathe Horizontally

Horizontal breathing is a popular breathing technique to help you expand your patience when you're "narrowing in." Narrowing in is when you get too invested in a current difficulty, including feeling impatient, and you no longer have the broader, more optimistic perspective you usually do.

Instead of staying narrowed in, try this exercise to force your body *and* your mind to refocus on expansion.

1. Stand up or sit comfortably upright, with your back straight. Make sure your abdomen doesn't feel compressed.
2. As you begin your next inhale, think about expanding your rib cage horizontally rather than vertically. Try to expand your lungs outward instead of upward.
3. When you exhale, reverse the process. Try to draw your navel and your ribs in toward your core. Repeat for at least a few minutes, filling your lungs completely and emptying them completely.

While you practice this technique, keep your mind on your breath. Notice how your mind starts to "expand" along with your breath. With this broadened attention and perspective, you'll find it much easier to choose patience.

Send a Beam of Positive Energy

This is a fun visualization to do as a break from any task that is making you feel impatient. It accomplishes two things at once: It reconnects you to the love and care you feel for another person, and it brings you a sense of peace and stillness that you can apply toward finding more patience for your current situation.

Here's how it works:

1. Find a comfortable spot to sit and close your eyes.
2. Take a deep breath in, filling your lungs completely, then let all the air out through your nostrils.
3. Settle in and focus your attention on one person; it should be someone who is very dear to you.
4. See that person in your mind's eye and concentrate on them. Gather up all the love, compassion, and care that you have for this person, and create a beam of positive energy to send to them.
5. Visualize the beam traveling the distance between where you are and where they are. Watch as it twists and turns on city streets, or send it straight through space and buildings alike to get to them.
6. See the beam as it reaches them. Imagine that they send you the same positive energy back through the same beam, making it even brighter and stronger. Soak in this positive energy for a few minutes.

With this positive energy absorbed into you, you'll return to your task with more compassion and patience.

✦

He that can have patience can have what he will.

—BENJAMIN FRANKLIN
American founding father

Use Only One Hand

This may be the ultimate exercise in humbleness, which means it has great potential to slow you down, re-evaluate your perspective, and inspire patience!

When you try a task with one hand when you would normally use two, you'll notice that it requires more time to think about what you're doing. You have to use more brainpower than you usually do to complete the task, which gives you an opportunity to glimpse a challenging experience beyond the things that typically make you impatient.

Here are a few tasks that you can try with one hand:

- Dressing yourself in the morning
- Washing your body and/or hair in the shower
- Squeezing toothpaste onto your toothbrush
- Cooking a meal
- Typing on a keyboard

While trying these tasks one-handed might make you feel momentarily frustrated, this impatience will morph into a deep focus, patience for yourself, and a brand-new perspective on how to tackle tasks that seemed so easy before.

Carry Something Heavy

This exercise is about realizing that anger, frustration, tension, stress, and impatience are heavy burdens that weigh just as heavily on you as physical burdens.

This exercise is a popular tactic also used by weight loss programs to show people how much weight they've lost so far, and to motivate them to continue. It's eye-opening to see how much weight you've been carrying, whether that's physical or emotional weight.

Here's what you do:

1. Find something around you that is annoying to carry but not too difficult. It should also be something that you don't need both hands to carry. If you can, find a way to strap it on, or carry it in a bag or backpack.
2. Once it's strapped on or secured, do your best to forget it's there and go on about your day.
3. Carry it while you do everyday tasks, like laundry, cooking, or cleaning. Try to carry it for at least thirty minutes or so to get the full effect.
4. When the time is up, notice how carrying this weight has affected you. Feel the extra tension or exhaustion in your muscles, the strain on your back or shoulders, and anything else that carrying this burden caused.
5. Now, put it down. Notice the feeling of relief and freedom that washes over you!

Recognize that shedding this physical weight was a good move, and decide to shed the emotional weight of impatience too.

Hold Your Breath

The simple act of holding your breath when you feel overwhelmed and impatient can encourage you to pause, slow down, and be more patient with yourself and your surroundings.

Here's how to do it:

1. When you notice you're feeling impatient—or when you just want to practice being more patient—pause what you're doing and sit still for a few moments.
2. Take in a deep breath through your nose, and exhale it all through your mouth, letting everything go.
3. Take in another slow, steady breath through your nose. When your lungs are full, stop and hold your breath. Time yourself to see how long you can hold it. Continue until just before it gets really uncomfortable, then let it all out in a big exhale.
4. Now, repeat the exercise but holding at a different point; after a slow, steady breath in and a full exhale, hold your breath with empty lungs. See how long you can hold it after an exhale.

Note how you feel afterward. You will likely feel a rush of gratitude for the amazing ability to breathe whenever and however you'd like! Let this gratitude pave the way toward more patience.

✦

Patience is not
the ability to wait.
Patience is to be
calm no matter what
happens, constantly
take action to turn
it to positive growth
opportunities, and
have faith to believe
that it will all work out
in the end while you
are waiting.

—ROY T. BENNETT
American author of The Light in the Heart

Breathe in Love, Breathe Out Peace

Breathing techniques are especially effective for boosting your patience, since they require you to set aside everything that is bothering you, including your past- and future-focused concerns. When you marry a breath technique with a positive emotion, it makes the exercise even *more* impactful, because you are effectively breathing in positivity *and* the current moment, leaving no room for negativity or outside factors that were making you feel impatient.

This exercise combines breath and positivity in a particularly pleasant way:

1. Find a comfortable space and sit down. Rest your hands on your knees and close your eyes.
2. Settle in with a few centering breaths, then pause for a moment. When you resume breathing, take slow and steady breaths.
3. As you breathe in, imagine you are breathing in all the love in the universe. You can feel it rushing in with the air, filling you with light, joy, and warmth.
4. As you breathe out, imagine you are breathing out pure peace. You are adding an immeasurable amount of peace to the world with every exhale, making it a calmer, more serene place.
5. Continue breathing this way for at least three minutes.

As you breathe in love and breathe out peace, you will build your innate capacity for patience. When you finish this exercise, you will have a well of peace to draw from when you want to choose patience.

Challenge Yourself with Tree Pose

Trees are wonderful examples of patience. They stand resiliently through different weather, seasons, and many, many years of life. Their growth isn't something that can be sped up; trees patiently, silently, and continuously grow at their own pace.

Emulate the strength and patience of trees with the Tree Pose. This pose helps you practice your balance, calm your heart rate, strengthen your legs and back, and stretch your legs, hips, and shoulders. In addition, it can provoke a strong centering effect, making you feel more at one with yourself and at peace with your surroundings.

Here's how to try Tree Pose:

1. Stand upright with your feet together and your arms at your sides. Bring your right knee up to your waist (or as high as it will go) while keeping your hips level. Try not to lean your hips out to the left.
2. Grab your right foot with your right hand and place it high up on your left inner thigh, with the sole of your right foot pressing into your left leg. If this is too difficult, you can place it against your left calf instead, or even keep it on the ground, but lean your right heel against your left ankle.
3. Find your balance here, then take your arms up overhead, placing your palms against one another.
4. Stay here for at least thirty seconds as you breathe calmly and slowly. Switch legs and repeat the exercise on the other side.

When you're feeling strong and centered after Tree Pose, you will have a greater capacity for patience.

Visualize a Cocoon

Humans don't spin their own cocoons like some insects do, but you can create a cocoon in your mind and spend some time relaxing, de-stressing, and enhancing your patience there.

Have you ever thought about how cozy a cocoon seems? Unless you have an aversion to small spaces, a cocoon probably seems like a pretty nice, warm, relaxing place to unwind!

Here's how:

1. Sit comfortably and close your eyes. Engage your imagination. Visualize a cocoon being woven around you. It's made of soft, flexible material, and it's beautiful to watch as it weaves back and forth, layering a custom-sized cocoon that fits you perfectly.
2. Inside this cocoon, you're warm and comfortable. Nothing can make its way inside to hurt or bother you.
3. Imagine yourself resting in this cocoon. See yourself completely relaxed and at ease, soaking in the coziness of the cocoon. Allow it to fill you with contentment and serenity.
4. Stay here for at least a few minutes, until you have absorbed all the good feelings you can, then gently emerge from the cocoon and open your eyes to continue your day.

Spending some time in a nice cozy cocoon—even an imaginary one—can give you the safe and secure feeling you need to approach your day with curiosity and patience rather than anxiety and impatience.

✦

Patience you must have, my young Padawan.

—YODA

Jedi and teacher from the Star Wars films

Laugh at Yourself

When you notice yourself acting impatiently such as tapping your foot or rolling your eyes, try laughing at yourself. Laughter is the best medicine, as they say, and laughing at yourself is even more beneficial for impatience! When you laugh at yourself, it means you refrain from taking yourself too seriously, and that you can recognize your own flaws and foibles, yet still feel ultimately positive about yourself. It's a great indicator of your mental state.

One of the greatest and most frequent opportunities you have to laugh at yourself is when you're feeling impatient. You'll turn that feeling of irritation completely on its head and into one of joy as you remind yourself that whatever you were feeling impatient about is actually not that serious.

Here's what to remind yourself of in order to turn the frustration into laughter:

- Impatience is when you get upset because the reality around you does not match how you think reality *should* be. It's pretty presumptuous to think that you know exactly how reality should be!
- The idea that you are upset with reality for not moving as fast as you'd like is sort of absurd when you stop to think about it. Being impatient is essentially throwing a fit because reality doesn't match your desired speed.

If you really absorb these two points, you'll see how silly it is to be angry and impatient over something—especially if it's something you have no control over.

Engage Your Whole Body

Impatience requires a forward focus, a nagging feeling that the future is not moving fast enough to meet you. When you are fully engaged in the present, the future has no bearing on you. One great way to focus in on the present moment is to use your whole body to embrace the now.

Here's how:

1. Wherever you are, find a private space. You can do this exercise sitting, standing, or lying down—whatever feels most comfortable for you.
2. When you're comfortable in your space and ready to begin, take in a deep breath.
3. As you breathe in, engage all the muscles in your body. Curl your toes inward, make fists with your hands, shrug your shoulders up, engage your abs, flex your legs, etc. Engage every muscle in your body that you can consciously control. Draw even your eyebrows in toward one another, and squeeze your eyes shut.
4. Hold here, with all your muscles squeezed and engaged, for five seconds. When you release your muscles, exhale and let everything go all at once.
5. Take a few deep, calming breaths, then do Steps 3 through 5 again. Repeat this exercise at least five times.

As you let go of your muscles and your breath the last time, you'll notice that you are completely engaged in the present moment, and that you feel a sense of relief and relaxation.

Look for a Silver Lining

Next time you feel impatient about a situation, try looking for a silver lining in the experience. The silver lining is the unintended and unexpected positive side effect of an unfortunate event or negative experience. There's a silver lining when you can say, "Well, what I wanted and hoped for didn't happen, but at least I got something positive out of it!"

When you look for a silver lining, you train your brain to scan your experience for the positive instead of drowning in the negative. You empower yourself to make the best of whatever life throws your way, which allows you to operate from a place of greater peace and patience.

When you're feeling impatient about something, here's how to look for a silver lining:

- Ask yourself, "What good thing would I be missing out on right now if I weren't in this uncomfortable or challenging situation?"
- Come up with an answer for yourself. If you can, come up with multiple answers. Some examples may include the simple opportunity to practice patience, the chance to chat with someone you wouldn't normally talk to, or even the gift of time to do work on something else while you wait.

Build some gratitude for the silver linings, and use them as a reminder that it's always good to have the opportunity to practice patience.

Spark Some Joy

Most likely, you would characterize impatience as a joyless emotion. Try sparking joy to defeat impatience when you feel it starting to manifest.

If you've heard anything about organizer extraordinaire Marie Kondo, you've probably heard her signature question: "Does it spark joy?" She encourages people to ask this question when they hold an item that they're considering getting rid of; if the answer is yes, they keep it. If the answer is no, they donate it, recycle it, or toss it.

You don't need to make tough decisions or embrace minimalism right now, but you can put that idea of sparking joy to good use. Follow these steps:

1. Find an item in your home that you really love, something that you enjoy looking at or using on a regular basis. Pick it up (or put your hands on it if it's too heavy to pick up).
2. As you hold it, feel some of the joy that's stored in the item transferring to you. Allow that spark of joy to grow and flourish inside of you. Feel the smile spread on your face.
3. As you put it down, ask yourself how you're feeling right now. Is there any room left for feeling angry or impatient when you've sparked joy?

You're probably feeling pretty full with the joy! Remember this easy exercise the next time you're struggling with feeling angry or impatient.

✦

Patience and diligence, like faith, remove mountains.

—WILLIAM PENN
English writer and founder of the colony of Pennsylvania

Put the Extra Time to Good Use

If you are waiting on something to happen and feel impatient about it, one good way to be more patient is to find a productive use for the time between now and the event. In modern everyday life, most people feel busy and overwhelmed more than they feel at peace, or even bored. Decide to change your perspective on waiting, and use the extra time in a productive way!

Here are some potential ways you can use the extra time between now and the event you are waiting for:

- Clean or organize the space you are currently in.
- Pay some bills.
- Check your bank account or balance your checkbook.
- Read a chapter or two from a book you've been meaning to start.
- Do a quick workout or yoga session.
- Get back to someone who reached out to you.

This list offers some examples, but it's really endless; you can find a myriad of productive ways to fill up time when you're impatient, whether it's just for five minutes or a few hours.

Make Yourself Wait

If you want to enhance your own patience, here's an effective and simple way to do it: Make yourself wait!

Most people are not thrilled by this idea, and that's because people are so used to getting things quickly these days that it's almost foreign to have to wait. You might not like waiting in general, and making your waiting self-imposed is even harder.

It's an uncomfortable and even challenging practice, but it's a really impactful one. Follow these instructions to start making yourself wait:

1. At least once a day, pick something that you're looking forward to doing or eager to get done. Decide when you would ideally like to engage in this task or activity.
2. Build in some purposeful wait time. Choose a time that is appropriate to the event. For example, if you're excited to see a new movie that comes out in a month, decide on waiting for a day or two after it's released. If you're looking forward to sinking onto the couch and watching TV, decide to take fifteen or twenty more minutes to work on your current task instead.

When your wait time is over, notice that you're even more excited and happy to engage in the activity or event you were looking forward to. You'll also find that you can tolerate longer waiting periods over time.

Take the Long Way Around

When you remember to appreciate your time on the (physical or metaphorical) road, you leave much less room for impatience to sprout and grow. Whether you call it taking the long way around or taking the scenic route, there's something to be said for choosing the longer or more difficult road. In this world of shortcuts and optimized routes, you can easily forget to enjoy the journey as well as the destination.

Here's what to do:

1. The next time you're headed somewhere, whether it's on foot or by car or any other mode of transportation, take a look at your options.
2. Instead of defaulting to the shortest or most direct route, think about the different routes available to you. Note the pros and cons of each route, including time, distance, sights, and smells (if one route takes you by a bakery, you probably want to prioritize that route).
3. Choose a route that you don't normally take, and set off down your path.
4. Notice all the pros about this route that you identified earlier. Experience the sights, the smells, and any other positive experiences this route provides that the others didn't. Appreciate this unique and wonderful route.

The more often you take the scenic or long way around, the more tolerant you will be of your impatience and perceived inconveniences.

There's no advantage to hurrying through life.

—MASASHI KISHIMOTO
Japanese manga artist behind Naruto

Determine What's Really Important

If you feel like you don't have enough time to get through your tasks, you're likely to feel impatient. You might think to yourself, "If only I had more time in the day!"

Today's world reinforces constant productivity, but this isn't conducive to your mental health or eliminating impatience.

Instead of wishing you had more time there's another secret option: You can determine what's really important and drop things that don't matter.

Here's how:

1. Make a list of the many things you do each day. Include work, chores, things you do for your household, things you do with friends and family, etc.
2. Now take a look at this list and think about what is really important. Work is important, because it provides your means of living and paying bills, but are there things you do that you don't necessarily need to? Similarly, seeing friends and family is important, but are there any engagements where you feel drained and exhausted instead of happy and loved after?
3. Determine which things are really important and which are not. Decide to do less of the things that are not important.

It's a long process, but you'll have more time in the day and less reason to become impatient when you're finished.

Make a List of Your Impatience Triggers

Everyone experiences things that trigger impatience. While you may associate the word "trigger" with trauma, everyone has triggers toward certain thoughts, feelings, and behaviors.

If you don't know what triggers your impatience, you can't pinpoint why you suddenly feel agitated, and you might be compelled toward certain unhealthy behaviors—like snapping at a loved one—without even knowing why. When you figure out what your triggers are, you can start to take more responsibility for yourself and your life, creating an environment of self-direction instead of passivity.

Here's how to figure out what your triggers are when it comes to impatience:

1. Sit down with your notebook and something to write with. Think about the times when you are most likely to become impatient. For example, you might be most likely to feel impatient in traffic or in a waiting room.
2. Determine what it is about these scenarios that makes you feel so impatient. Is it feeling out of control? Is it waiting on others? Or perhaps it's when you don't have something productive to do?
3. Figure out what features trigger your impatience and write them down.

Now that you know your triggers, you have options: You can plan your day in such a way as to avoid these triggers, or you can work on making these triggers less "triggering." Either way, you're building yourself a more patient environment.

Create Your Own Patience Mantras

Mantras are a fabulous way of working on your self-development toward patience. You can use them to guide yourself toward your goal to be more patient by designing mantras that specifically target this key trait. When you create your own mantras, make sure they feel personally relevant and meaningful to you so that they'll be more impactful.

Here's how to create your own patience mantras:

1. Think about what situations you want to practice more patience in (see the exercise on the previous page, Make a List of Your Impatience Triggers, if you need help identifying these situations).
2. Determine what reminder or idea would be most helpful in each situation. For example, if you get impatient during traffic, you might need to remind yourself that you're not in control and that you need to let go.
3. Now, create a mantra to match each situation. For the traffic example, you might use: *I can't control everything. Go with the flow.*

Take your new list of mantras for each situation with you. You can use these whenever the need arises.

✦

It is far better to endure patiently a smart which nobody feels but yourself, than to commit a hasty action whose evil consequences will extend to all connected with you.

—CHARLOTTE BRONTË
English novelist and poet

Practice Patience Affirmations

Affirmations can help you work toward many of your goals, and they can be particularly beneficial for building patience.

Affirmations are often confused with mantras, as they have a similar form and function, but they're two distinct tools. Mantras are about reminding yourself of a truth about the world, a theme, or a more abstract idea. Affirmations, on the other hand, are all about you: your capacity, your competence, your value, and your ability to do what you set your mind to. Affirmations for patience are sincere, heartfelt messages from you to you about the patient person you want to be.

Here's how to create and practice patience affirmations:

1. First, get out a pen and paper and write your own affirmations. They should be short, just a brief sentence or two at most. They should also be positive (e.g., "I am" instead of "I am not") and framed in the present (e.g., "I am" instead of "I will be"). Examples include *I choose patience* and *I am at peace within and without*.

2. Now that you have your affirmations, carry them with you. You can take the piece of paper with you, copy them on a sticky note, save them to your phone, or use any other method to make them easily available.

3. At least a few times a day (in the morning, at night, and in difficult moments), take out your affirmations and practice them. Say them out loud to yourself, preferably in the mirror.

Practice for just a few days and you'll start to see yourself be more patient in every situation!

Engage Your Empathy

When you feel irritated and impatient with someone, you might feel wrapped up in your own experience. In those moments of impatience, you are stuck in your own thoughts and feelings, and you might struggle to understand and identify with others. Not only is this a negative and disconnecting state to be in, you're also cut off from one way out of impatience: empathy.

It's tough to be empathetic when someone is making you feel impatient, but it's also the key to building your character and enhancing your capacity for patience.

Here's how to engage your empathy:

1. In a moment where you are feeling impatient because of another person, notice what is happening and hit the "pause button" on the experience (e.g., take a break, stop and think, journal for a few minutes).
2. Think about how the other person is feeling right now. Don't just assume you know how they feel and move on. Instead of judging or dismissing the way you think they might feel, allow yourself to truly feel it.
3. Spend a few moments empathizing, then pull back into your own present moment. Think about how you'd like to respond now that you have some understanding of what they're feeling.

You'll likely notice that you feel more positively about this person and more patient about the situation after empathizing. This is a difficult but important way to practice patience.

✦

Knowing trees, I understand the meaning of patience. Knowing grass, I can appreciate persistence.

—HAL BORLAND
American author, journalist, and naturalist

Practice Radical Acceptance

Most of the time spent feeling impatient or frustrated is born out of the discrepancy between how things actually are, and how you think they "should be." When you are able to let go of this strict idea of what "should be," you give yourself permission to live fully in the real world, where you can create realistic expectations that help you instead of hurt you.

Radical acceptance is, as you might guess from the name, a radical idea: that you can choose to accept reality exactly as you find it, no matter how far that is from what you would like it to be or what you think it should be.

Here's how to practice radical acceptance:

1. In any given moment (but especially when X thing is causing you to feel impatient), remind yourself that this is your current reality.
2. In your current reality, acknowledge that X is happening. Acknowledge that it's uncomfortable or unpleasant.
3. Let go of any idea about whether X should be happening or not happening, or how, where, or when it should be happening. Shed these expectations and accept that X is happening in front of you, right now.
4. Say to yourself, "It's okay that X is happening."

That's it! That's all there is to radical acceptance. It's establishing a baseline for accepting the reality of your life. You don't have to like it, but accepting it is the only way to cope, address, or move past feelings of impatience.

Play "Five Years from Now"

When you are impatient, your perspective narrows: You see only your own woes. When you choose patience, you broaden your perspective to see the positive in your own experiences and the full spectrum of things happening outside of your narrow view.

This is a fun and easy game called "Five Years from Now." It's designed to give you perspective on your current situation and to help you choose patience. It's meant to be played by yourself, although you can incorporate other players if you'd like.

Here's how to play the game:

1. Grab some paper and a pen in case you want to write during the game.
2. Either write out or ask yourself the question, "In five years from now, will this matter?"
3. Put yourself in your own shoes, five years from now. Imagine yourself walking around, enjoying your life. Ask yourself whether your current frustration matters to this version of you. Write down your answer.
4. If the answer is no (and it almost always is), allow yourself to let it go. Let the problem or issue slide off of you like rain off an umbrella.
5. If the answer is yes, give yourself some compassion and determine the best way to mitigate the damage.

Generally, you will find that your current problems will not matter in five years. Use this game to remind yourself of what really matters and let go of your impatience.

✦

If you are patient in one moment of anger, you will escape a hundred days of sorrow.

—RAINER MARIA RILKE
Bohemian-Austrian poet and novelist

Find a Patience Model

Everyone has strengths and weaknesses when it comes to patience. Some can be completely Zen in situations where others would tear their hair out, and vice versa.

This means that whenever you're ready to tear your hair out, there's likely at least one person you can think of who would exude patient Zen vibes in the same situation. You can look to this person for support, encouragement, and inspiration.

If you're feeling impatient, try finding a patience model. Here's what to do:

1. Think back over the past few weeks and try to remember when you witnessed someone being patient. Maybe you saw a mother being patient with a toddler tantrum at a store, or two dog owners patiently calming their excited dogs. It may take some scanning of your recent memories, but you're bound to find at least one person.
2. Revisit that moment in as much detail as possible. See how patient they looked, and imagine how patient they were feeling inside.
3. Adopt this person as your personal model of patience in this moment. Try to shift your experience and your outward presentation to match theirs. Strive to look and feel as patient as they did.

This exercise rolls many helpful techniques (including observation, empathy, and connection, among others) into one, providing a big boost to your ability and willingness to choose patience.

There is one form of hope which is never unwise, and which certainly does not diminish with the increase of knowledge. In that form it changes its name, and we call it patience.

—EDWARD GEORGE BULWER-LYTTON
English writer and politician

Index